Apollinaire
and the Faceless Man

Apollinaire and the Faceless Man
The Creation and Evolution of a Modern Motif

Willard Bohn

Rutherford • Madison • Teaneck
Fairleigh Dickinson University Press
London and Toronto: Associated University Presses

© 1991 by Associated University Presses, Inc.

All rights reserved. Authorization to photocopy items for internal or personal use, or the internal or personal use of specific clients, is granted by the copyright owner, provided that a base fee of $10.00, plus eight cents per page, per copy is paid directly to the Copyright Clearance Center, 27 Congress Street, Salem, Massachusetts 01970. [0-8386-3416-8/91 $10.00+8¢ pp, pc.]

Associated University Presses
440 Forsgate Drive
Cranbury, NJ 08512

Associated University Presses
25 Sicilian Avenue
London WC1A 2QH, England

Associated University Presses
P.O. Box 39, Clarkson Pstl. Stn.
Mississauga, Ontario
Canada L5J 3X9

The paper used in this publication meets the requirements
of the American National Standard for Permanence of Paper
for Printed Library Materials Z39.48-1984.

Library of Congress Cataloging-in-Publication Data

Bohn, Willard, 1939–
  Apollinaire and the faceless man : the creation and evolution of a modern motif / Willard Bohn.
      p.   cm.
  Includes bibliographical references and index.
  ISBN 0-8386-3416-8 (alk. paper)
  1. Apollinaire, Guillaume, 1880–1918—Criticism and interpretation. 2. Apollinaire, Guillaume, 1880–1918—Influence. 3. Surrealism (Literature)—France. 4. Face in literature. 5. Art and literature. 6. Face in art. 7. Surrealism. I. Title.
PQ2601.P6Z573   1991
841'.912—dc20   90-55161
                                                                    CIP

PRINTED IN THE UNITED STATES OF AMERICA

To my wife, Anita

Contents

Acknowledgments 9

1. Introduction 13
2. Apollinaire's Mysterious Musician 16
3. A Train Leaves for Paris 41
4. Alberto Savinio at Home 77
5. Giorgio de Chirico among the Mannequins 96
6. The Dawn of a New Age 132
7. Conclusion 151

Notes 155
Bibliography 167
Index 173

Acknowledgments

It is virtually impossible to acknowledge every institution and every individual who aided me, in one way or another, in the preparation of the following study. Nevertheless I would like to extend my gratitude in particular to Michel Décaudin and to Joseph J. Duggan, whose constant advice and encouragement were greatly appreciated as this project gradually took shape. Together with Thomas Parkinson and Ann Smock, they read the preliminary drafts and offered numerous constructive comments.

I am grateful as well to the following for the various roles they played in facilitating my research: to Mrs. Elizabeth Wrigley, the Director of The Francis Bacon Library, for permission to reproduce the Apollinaire manuscripts belonging to that institution and for help in this connection that went far beyond the call of duty. To the late Georgia O'Keeffe, Rodrigo de Zayas, and Yale University for allowing me to examine and to publish excerpts from letters in the Alfred Stieglitz Archive, Collection of American Literature, Beinecke Rare Book and Manuscript Library, Yale University. To Donald Gallup, Curator of the above collection, for his invaluable advice and efforts in this regard. To the late James Thrall Soby for advice concerning Giorgio de Chirico. To William Camfield for advice and for allowing me to examine various documents connected with Marius de Zayas, Francis Picabia, and the "291" group. To these names should be added those of P. M. Adéma and Gilbert Boudar, who also provided key information during the investigative phase of the study.

I would also like to thank the Museum of Modern Art (New York), the Solomon R. Guggenheim Museum (New York), the San Francisco Museum of Modern Art, the Musée National d'Art Moderne (Paris), the Wadsworth Atheneum (Hartford, Connecticut), the Yale University Art Gallery, the Kunstsammlung Nordrhein-Westfalen (Düsseldorf), and the Staatliche Museen zu Berlin (Nationalgalerie), which granted permission to reproduce paintings by Giorgio de Chirico and Paul Delvaux belonging to their collections. The former works appear by agreement with the copyright holder, © Giorgio de Chirico/VAGA New York 1990.

It remains to express my gratitude to the Graduate Division, University of California at Berkeley, for a grant at the beginning of this project and to the Graduate School, Illinois State University, for help in preparing my findings for publication in English. Several chapters have appeared previously, in a different form, in *Comparative Literature, Comparative Literature Studies,* and *Comparative Drama*. The volume itself was originally published in French by Bulzoni Editore in Rome. In the course of translating it into English I have revised various sections to reflect recent scholarship in those areas.

Apollinaire
and the Faceless Man

1
Introduction

The present work owes its existence to the discovery of an unknown pantomime by Guillaume Apollinaire entitled *A quelle heure un train partira-t-il pour Paris?* (What Time Does A Train Leave For Paris?). Written in 1914, the latter features a faceless flute-player whose enigmatic voyage through an ancient quarter of Paris is juxtaposed with a worldwide slice of life. Readers who are already familiar with Apollinaire will recognize the plot of "Le Musicien de Saint-Merry," a poem that antedates the pantomime by at least six months. Published in *Les Soirées de Paris* on 15 February 1914, it was probably composed during the preceding year. It is in this work that one encounters the faceless man and his mysterious entourage for the first time. Not only does his appearance mark a decisive point in the poet's career but it signals the introduction of an important motif into western art and literature. For reasons that no one could have foreseen—mostly associated with the First World War—the faceless man would soon come to symbolize the human condition. Closely linked to modern history, and to modern sensibility, he was to be adopted by writers and artists as a symbol of twentieth-century existence.

Among other things, this explains the great success of the motif and its universal attraction. In less than ten years, of which five were interrupted by the war, the faceless man became a citizen of the world. An important character in France, Italy, and Germany, he was to be found in every European country and was preparing to invade England and the United States. From Spain, where he had several partisans, he gained South America, settling first in Argentina and then in Mexico. By 1924, when André Breton published his first Surrealist manifesto, the faceless man had already become a universal motif.

It remained for Breton to officially recognize his importance and to establish him as a patron saint of Surrealism. Under the aegis of this movement the faceless man would acquire great popularity and would invade other continents. At the present moment—

nearly eighty years after its creation—the motif has lost none of its vitality. Often employed by the neo-Dadaists, it is still seen in Surrealist writing and art and occurs in numerous other contexts. A few years ago, during an exhibition of Yugoslavian prints at Brandeis University, I was surprised to encounter a whole series of works devoted to the faceless man. Reduced to an abstract bust and divided into quarters by two lines as if by the cross-hairs of a telescope, he was still perfectly recognizable. In fact the artist had drawn his inspiration from the Italian artist Giorgio Morandi, whose characters stem in turn from the Metaphysical School of Giorgio de Chirico and Carlo Carrá. It will be seen as the present study progresses that a previously unsuspected link exists between the *scuola metafisica* and Apollinaire. More recently the American painter Jedd Garet has revived much of de Chirico's iconography. In his paintings, which include souvenirs of de Chirico, Max Ernst, and Edvard Munch, the faceless man occupies the place of honor. By turns a domestic, a pirate, or the last representative of the human race, he reassures us and menaces us simultaneously.[1]

To study the faceless man in all his manifestations, both historic and geographical, would necessitate several volumes. I have preferred instead to analyze one period in detail in order to determine the motif's fundamental symbolism. This period embraces the years 1913–1919 and includes several metamorphoses before the motif was absorbed into the general aesthetic current. The first section of this study is devoted to the creation of the faceless man and to his various manifestations in Apollinaire's work. The second section examines the motif's impact on the artists and writers surrounding Apollinaire. Among the latter were Francis Picabia, Alberto Savinio, and Giorgio de Chirico, who employed the motif to different degrees. Marius de Zayas's presence is explained by the fact that, like Picabia and Savinio, he was a collaborator on *A quelle heure un train partira-t-il pour Paris?* The history of his collaboration is closely linked to that of the pantomime and constitutes a new chapter in the American avant-garde. The founder of Metaphysical Art, de Chirico was to play a key role in the Surrealist movement and would influence several generations of painters. Picabia was also to become a force to be reckoned with in avant-garde circles. In his role as artist, poet, and the director of several reviews, he helped determine the character of Dada and to revolutionize modern aesthetics. The last member, Savinio, was destined to become an important figure in the Italian avant-garde for a period of nearly forty years.

Situated at the junction of multple aesthetic currents, the faceless man evolved in different directions. His strategic location assured that he would be adopted by numerous schools and shaped according to their particular needs. Ironically this process was accelerated by the same forces that put an end to artistic life in Paris. After the war broke out, the members of the group who were experimenting with the motif dispersed to other countries (except for Apollinaire, who joined the army). There they contributed to the motif's expansion by exposing other poets and painters to their experiments. Although his postwar history exceeds the scope of the present study, the faceless man's attraction may be understood from his Parisian phase. Subsequent generations were to reinterpret him in ways that Apollinaire would never have dreamed of, but their emotional response would remain the same. Throughout his history, from one end to the other, the faceless man has exercised a strange fascination on his audience. In many respects the latter's reaction can be characterized as religious including an element of fear as well as an element of respect. An eminent figure in the drama of life and death, the faceless man continues to arouse intense emotions in readers and spectators alike.

2
Apollinaire's Mysterious Musician

The Musician of Saint-Merry

    At last I have the right to greet unfamiliar beings
    They pass before me and gather in the distance
    While everything about them is strange
    And their hope is no less strong than mine
5   I sing not of this world nor of other stars
      I sing the possibilities of myself beyond this world and the stars
      I sing the joy of wandering and the pleasure of a wanderer's death

    The 21st day of the month of May 1913
    Ferryman of the dead and swarming Merry-widows
10 Millions of flies were fanning a splendor
    When a man with no eyes no nose and no ears
    Leaving the Sébasto turned into the rue Aubry-le-Boucher
    The young man was dark with a strawberry blush on his cheeks
    Man Oh! Ariadne
15 He was playing the flute and the music guided his steps
    He halted at the corner of the rue Saint-Martin
    Playing the tune I am singing and which I invented

    All the women in his vicinity gathered near him
    They came from every direction
20 When Saint-Merry's bells suddenly began to ring
    The musician stopped playing and drank from the fountain
    Which is at the corner of the rue Simon-le-Franc
    Then Saint-Merry fell silent
    The stranger resumed his melody on the flute
25 And retracing his steps walked as far as the rue de la Verrerie
    Which he entered followed by the flock of women
    Who were coming out of the houses
    Who were coming out of the side streets with wild eyes
    Hands stretched toward the melodious ravisher

30 Unconcerned he strolled along playing his tune
He strolled along terribly

And elsewhere
What time does a train leave for Paris?

At that moment
35 Pigeons were leaving nutmeg droppings in the Moluccas
At the same time
Catholic mission in Boma what have you done with the sculptor

Elsewhere
She crosses a bridge connecting Bonn and Beuel and disappears in the direction of Pützchen

40 At the same moment
A girl in love with the mayor

In another quarter
So emulate oh poet the labels of perfume-makers

In short oh mockers you have not gotten a great deal out of men
45 And you have barely extracted a little grease from their misery
But we who are dying because we live so far apart
Stretch out our arms and along these rails rolls a long freight train

Seated next to me you were crying in the back of a horse-drawn cab

And now
50 You resemble me unhappily you resemble me

We resemble each other as in the architecture of the last century
Those tall chimneys shaped like towers
We are going higher now and no longer touch the ground

And while the world was living and fluctuating

55 The procession of women long as a day without bread
Followed the lucky musician in the rue de la Verrerie

Processions oh processions
When long ago the king would leave for Vincennes

When the ambassadors would come to Paris
60 When the meager Suger hastened toward the Seine
When the rioting died out around Saint-Merry

Processions oh processions
So numerous were the women that they overflowed
Into all the neighboring streets
65 Hurrying swift as a bullet
To follow the musician
Oh! Ariadne and you Pâquette and you Amine
And you Mia and you Simone and you Mavise
And you Colette and you lovely Geneviève
70 They passed by trembling and vain
And their quick light steps moved in cadence
To the pastoral music which guided
Their eager ears

The stranger stopped a moment before a house for sale
75 An abandoned house
With broken windows
A sixteenth-century dwelling
With delivery trucks parked in the courtyard
The musician proceeded to enter
80 His music as it grew fainter became languorous
The women followed him into the abandoned house
And all of them entered together in a group
All all entered without a backward glance
Without regretting what they had left behind
85 What they had abandoned
Without regretting light life or memory
Soon no one was left in the rue de la Verrerie
But myself and a priest from Saint-Merry
We entered the old house
90 But we found no one there

It is evening
At Saint-Merry the Angelus is ringing
Processions oh processions
When long ago the king would return from Vincennes
95 There came a troop of hatters
There came some banana pedlars
There came some Republican Guardsmen
Oh night
Flock of languorous feminine glances
100 Oh night
You my sorrow and my vain expectation
I hear the sound of a flute dying away in the distance.

Structure and Thematics

Although "Le Musicien de Saint-Merry" was first published in 1914, and later included in *Calligrammes* (1918), it has taken half a century for the poem to receive the scholarly recognition it deserves. This is surprising since the Surrealists valued the poem highly, and their works contain numerous allusions to the musician. André Breton and his associates were fascinated by Apollinaire's protagonist, the enigmatic "man with no eyes no nose and no ears," whom they associated with the mannequins in Giorgio de Chirico's paintings. In their opinion both characters epitomized *le merveilleux* ("the marvelous"), which was one of the central principles of Surrealist activity. Only recently, however, have critics begun to realize what an extraordinary work "Le Musicien de Saint-Merry" really is.[1] "Uno de los poemas más turbadores y misteriosos de Apollinaire" ("one of Apollinaire's most mysterious and disturbing poems") according to Octavio Paz, it is noteworthy for its complexity of conception and beauty of execution. Despite its fragmentary appearance recent critics have praised Apollinaire's unity of organization and inspiration. Antoine Fongaro aptly characterizes the poem as "la synthèse extraordinaire d'une foule d'éléments les plus hétéroclites" ("an extraordinary synthesis of a group of widely disparate elements").[2] Seen as a narrative *récit*, the poem's surface structure is symmetrical and regular.[3] Consisting of three movements and three "digressions" of varying lengths, "Le Musicien de Saint-Merry" was constructed according to the principle of ring composition. The actual sequence of scenes is the following:

Prologue	Story	Interlude	Story	Interlude	Story	Epilogue	Interlude	Epilogue
vv. 1–7	vv. 8–31	vv. 32–53	vv. 54–56	vv. 57–61	vv. 62–90	vv. 91–92	vv. 93–97	vv. 98–102
(7)	(24)	(22)	(3)	(5)	(29)	(2)	(5)	(5)

With two exceptions the different sections are arranged symmetrically about one central scene—the first interlude. The prologue and epilogue are the same length (7 lines) and balance each other perfectly. The same symmetry obtains in the long narrative sequence devoted to the story (vv. 8–90), where the parts before and after the first interlude also balance each other (24 lines versus 32 lines). Thus the outer prologue / epilogue frame of the poem is mirrored in the division of the story into beginning and end sections, which in turn provide a frame for the first interlude.

1. Guillaume Apollinaire on August 2, 1914.

The last two interludes are much shorter. Although they are inserted asymmetrically into the general pattern, they are symmetrical with respect to each other. Not only are they the same length but they are parallel in structure. The lines "Processions oh processions / When long ago the king would leave for Vincennes" evoke the answering lines "Processions oh processions / When long ago the king would return from Vincennes." Both are followed by three anaphoric lines beginning with "when" and "there came" respectively.

The narrative cohesiveness of "Le Musicien de Saint-Merry" is matched by a similar cohesion at the thematic level as well. The key themes, for example, are stated at the beginning and end and form an additional set of frames for the central episode. Some of the thematic statements are parallel, others follow a pattern of question and response. Thus the poem opens with the introduction of the mysterious flute music (v. 15) and closes with its disintegration (v. 102), paralleling the appearance and disappearance of the musician and his followers. Similarly, the bells of the Saint-Merry church are heard both at the beginning (v. 20) and at the end (v. 92). The initial hope of the narrator (v. 4), frustrated by the events of the poem, is transformed into "vain expectation" at the end (v. 101). The theme of death, introduced in verse 7, is restated in the very last line. The "beings" who "gather in the distance" in verse 2 are balanced by "the sound of a flute . . . in the distance" (v. 102). The intimate declarations of the narrator at the beginning (vv. 1–7) are answered by similar statements in the final couplet. In addition, there are both initial and terminal processions (vv. 2 and 93 ff.). As important as these frames are, however, they are not the only source of unity. An equally strong cohesiveness results from the complex system of cross-references throughout the work. Nothing is left to chance, everything is meticulously ordered. "Le Musicien de Saint-Merry" is fragmentary only in the sense that it resembles a collage—a collage whose elements are held together by the glue of symmetry and reflexive reference. It is "un univers . . . créé de toutes pièces" ("a patchwork universe"), to quote Apollinaire in a different context, and it is noteworthy that he was conscious of similarities between his technique and Picasso's.[4] Finally, it should be noted that Apollinaire's policy of omitting punctuation adds to the agglutinative process, since each line tends to adhere to the line above and below it.

It remains to mention the theme of the *cortège* ("procession"), which recurs throughout the poem. Besides the refrain "Cortèges ô cortèges," which is heard at three different times, there are eight additional references to processions. These are accompanied by other evocations of linear progression: images of trains in motion (twice), of someone crossing a bridge, of outstretched arms, and of a melody fading away in the distance. To be sure, processional imagery plays an important role in Apollinaire's poetry in general (cf. "Cortège" and "La Maison des morts"). In "Le Musicien de Saint-Merry" the central procession represents a variation on what S. I. Lockerbie has termed "le thème du vagabondage" ("the wanderer theme"), which structures Apollinaire's most famous poem "Zone."[5] Indeed traces of the latter theme are also to be found in the present poem (e.g., v. 7: "I sing the joy of wandering . . ."). Among other things the linear progression of the faceless man and his women provides considerable momentum, paralleling the experience of the reader as he progresses from beginning to end. Significantly, the meter is based on the alexandrine, whose slower rhythm corresponds to the deliberate advancement of the *cortège*, which is halted by a rhyming couplet at the very end.

The rhythm of the advancing procession is interrupted three times by apparently extraneous interludes. Here the chronological time of the narrative, which is essentially linear or horizontal, yields to a subjective time that may be pictured as vertical. Reproducing the simultaneous nature of reality, they evoke both the universal passage of life and—in Paz's words—"ese continuo fluir de pensamientos, sensaciones y memorias que se agolpan a las puertas de nuestra conciencia a cada segundo" ("that continual flux of thoughts, feelings, and memories that pound on the doors of our consciousness every second"). At one level, then, the interludes reflect the flow of Apollinaire's consciousness, both as narrator and as protagonist, during the course of the poem/procession. Moreover, Apollinaire distinguishes between spatial and temporal simultanism. The last two interludes are devoted to the latter, comprising a series of historical vignettes. The first interlude evokes events occurring all over the world to create a global slice of life (cf. v. 54: "And while the world was living and fluctuating").

Among the heterogeneous elements collected together in this section, "What time does a train leave for Paris?" (v. 33) evokes a conversation in a provincial railroad station. The pigeons of the Moluccas, or Spice Islands, whose diet consists of nutmegs (v. 35), have been chosen for their exoticism.[6] The same is undoubtedly true of the line "Catholic mission in Boma what have you done with the sculptor" (v. 37), representing an unspoken question in Apollinaire's mind, but here several additional factors are at work. As Philippe Renaud remarks, it constitutes "une prise de position à la fois idéologique et esthétique" ("both an aesthetic and an ideological stance").[7] Apollinaire opposes the missionaries in the Belgian Congo (of which Boma was the capital) to the African sculptors under their jurisdiction for two reasons. First of all, he is attacking the imposition of Christianity on the African populace in general. In eradicating African culture and replacing it with its European counterpart, the missionaires were in effect destroying the people they were supposed to be saving. The Catholic mission in the Congo seems to have been particularly autocratic and was continually embroiled in disputes with the colonial administration.[8] Second, Apollinaire is deploring the eradication of African art. A convert to Christianity, the sculptor can no longer carve masks and statues depicting his tribal gods. Since this is the only art form available to him, he has no choice but to renounce his profession.

The theme of African art is linked to another line in the first interlude: "So emulate oh poet the labels of perfume-makers" (v. 43). This is a silent exhortation by Apollinaire to his fellow practitioners. Just as African sculpture was influencing modern painting at the time, labels and posters were inspiring modern poetry (cf. "Zone"). These two contemporary themes are complemented by two additional motifs: machinery and industrialization. The image of the train in line 47 is echoed by that of an airplane a few lines later: "We are going higher now and no longer touch the ground" (v. 53). That the "tall chimneys shaped like towers" (v. 52) include at least one factory smokestack will also become evident. Finally, the first interlude contains several references to women that will be discussed later in another context.

Structure and Plot

The plot of "Le Musicien de Saint-Merry" is deceptively simple. Strolling through the streets of the Marais district of Paris, a faceless flute-player attracts hordes of women who follow him into an abandoned house—where they disappear into thin air. For all its simplicity, however, the poem remains stubbornly resistant to interpretation. This is because its meaning depends on a series of interlocking structures buried far beneath the surface. Arranged in a crystalline pattern, these deep structures consist of a seemingly endless series of verticals and horizontals, each of which is reflected in the others. The poem itself is constructed around an autobiographical center. Not only does it stem from personal experience; it magnifies this experience and projects it onto a number of different levels where it undergoes some startling transformations. Throughout the work the driving force is the poet's desire for revenge, motivated partly by his recent breakup with the painter Marie Laurencin. As Apollinaire's rage struggles to burst its poetic bonds it is restrained—and eventually contained—by two structural devices: the figure of the *cortège* and the creation of narrative multiplicity. The point of departure and the destination of the former coincide with the beginning and end of the poem. Proceeding along a carefully chosen route, leading from the boulevard de Sébastopol to the ominous house, the procession defines the poem's horizontal boundaries. In addition the linear voyage in space suggests a parallel voyage in *time*. In this second instance, which traverses the domains of autobiography, history, and psychology, one encounters multiple narratives that are superimposed on each other to form a series of structural parallels. These determine the vertical limits of the poem and are the source of its ultimate meaning. Consigned to this syntagmatic and paradigmatic cage, Apollinaire's rage activates successive levels of signification ranging from the personal to the universal, from the particular to the general. As Michel Décaudin observes, "on passe dans 'Le Musicien' d'une réalité vécue, chronologiquement située, à quelque chose qui est de l'ordre du mythe" ("In 'Le Musicien' we go from everyday reality, situated chronologically, to something bordering on myth").[9] In making this transition, as will be seen, one passes through at least eleven different levels. Some of these are of major importance; others are relatively minor.

The Superficial Story

One notes first of all that the poem recounts a supernatural occurrence that is meant to mystify the reader. The aura of mystery is intensified by the precision of the references. Thus Apollinaire gives the exact itinerary of the procession, street by street, which can easily be retraced on any pre-1934 map of Paris. In a similar vein he gives the precise date of the supposed encounter: "The 21st day of the month of May 1913."

Prostitutes and Client

"Le Musicien de Saint-Merry" incorporates three additional processions that are rooted in contemporary reality. Critics agree, for instance, that the mysterious women are in fact prostitutes residing in the area. For one thing, this quarter was infested with *filles de joie* and associated hoodlums in Apollinaire's day, and had been since the Middle Ages.[10] For another, the list of women enumerated *à la François Villon* (vv. 67–69) is headed by Ariadne, who appears as a prostitute in another poem ("Arbre").[11] It is generally agreed that the words "mordonnantes mériennes" (v. 9) designate the local prostitutes *(mériennes)*, who confer *la petite mort (mort donnant)* via sexual intercourse. Thus the poem may be seen as depicting a group of prostitutes in pursuit of a potential customer, perhaps even Apollinaire.

The Bakers' Strike

Marc Poupon has discovered that in May 1913 the Parisian bakers, headquartered in the Saint-Merry district since the Middle Ages, went on strike. Two bakeries remained open in the rue de la Verrerie and were swamped by customers—until their windows were broken by strikers. Poupon suggests that Apollinaire transformed the long queues of housewives waiting for bread into his procession, which among other things is "long as a day without bread" (v. 55). Not only do the broken windows in the bakeries echo the "vitres brisées" of the abandoned house—also in the rue de la Verrerie—but there was, and still is, a type of French bread called a *flûte*.

The Guided Tour

While the bread lines seem to have played a role in the elaboration of the poem, its actual genesis was provided by a different experience. In 1971 Pierre Caizergues discovered that on 4 May 1913 Apollinaire led a guided tour through the Saint-Merry district on behalf of the Société des Amis du Paris Pittoresque. Since then the notes he used for the tour have come to light.[12] Apollinaire's reasons for choosing the *cortège* as the basis of his poem, and for situating it in this area, were thus partly autobiographical. This explains why the poem exhibits such a detailed knowledge of the quarter. The faceless protagonist follows part of the route taken by Apollinaire two weeks before. From the boulevard de Sébastopol he enters the rue Aubry-le-Boucher and stops at the intersection of the rue Saint-Martin. Apollinaire undoubtedly halted his own procession to explain that on 5 June 1832 a terrible battle took place here during the popular insurrection that erupted on the occasion of General Lamarque's funeral. The widespread fighting, which involved most of the area, is commemorated by the line "When the rioting died out around Saint-Merry" (v. 61).[13] The next stop is the corner of the rue Saint-Martin and the rue Simon-le-Franc, where the hero drinks from a fountain. Apollinaire's notes reveal that he stopped here to point out the Fontaine Maubuée, dating from the thirteenth century, which was immortalized by François Villon in his *Testament* (stanza 105).[14]

The faceless man then walks in the opposite direction to the corner of the rue Saint-Martin and the rue de la Verrerie (the site of the Eglise de Saint-Merry) and proceeds down the latter street until he reaches the abandoned house, "a sixteenth-century dwelling." This is very possibly the building at 83 rue de la Verrerie, which dates from the sixteenth century and belonged to Bossuet's father. It is praised by all the guidebooks for its beautiful exposed staircase and is mentioned in Apollinaire's notes. The rectory of the Eglise de Saint-Merry across the street stands on the former site of the house belonging to "the meager Suger" (v. 60)—the abbé of Saint Denis who was counselor to Louis VI and Louis VII, an able diplomat, and the author of several histories.[15] It is appropriate that Apollinaire chose the rue de la Verrerie in which to evoke various historical processions: "When long ago the king would leave for Vincennes / When the ambassadors would come to Paris" and so forth. For, as he explained during his tour, Louis XIV widened the street in 1672 to facilitate his passage between the Louvre and his chateau at Vincennes and to serve "les ambassadeurs étrangers [qui] passaient par cette rue lors de leur entrée solennelle [à Paris]" ("the foreign ambassadors [who] made their solemn entry [into Paris] through this street").[16] Apollinaire obviously gleaned these details from a guidebook, but the hatters, banana pedlars, and Republican Guardsmen (vv. 95–97) are taken from personal observation. The quarter was sprinkled with fruit and clothing stores, and the Republican Guard had a barrack nearby.[17] Poupon suggests that the *casquettiers* are not cap-makers but cap-*wearers*, that is, pimps and hoodlums. He adds that the

Guardsmen are probably on leave and have come to patronize the prostitutes.

The Sexual Fantasy

Apollinaire treats this factual background material in two ways. By filtering it through his personal experience, he incorporates it into a psychological system. At the same time he gives it a mythic dimension through processes that will be examined later. In the first instance, it has long been recognized that Apollinaire is the hero of his own poem. He is present in three different guises: as the protagonist (musician), as the narrator (speaker), and as the poet (singer). The relations between these three *personae*, which are constantly shifting, are extremely complicated, but it is enough to note that the attributes of the first two are combined in the role of the third. Apollinaire is thus present both as observer and as participant—that is, as the embodiment of the different aspects of poetic creation.[18] This explains the puzzling statement that the faceless man is playing the very tune that Apollinaire is singing and that he invented (v. 17): they are one and the same person. The tune itself is described in the preceding lines:

J'ai enfin le droit de saluer des êtres que je ne connais pas
Ils passent devant moi et s'accumulent au loin
Tandis que tout ce que j'en vois m'est inconnu
Et leur espoir n'est pas moins fort que le mien

Je ne chante pas ce monde ni les autres astres
Je chante toutes les possibilités de moi-même hors de ce monde et des astres
Je chante la joie d'errer et le plaisir d'en mourir

(At last I have the right to greet unfamiliar beings
They pass before me and gather in the distance
While everything about them is strange
And their hope is no less strong than mine

I sing not of this world nor of other stars
I sing the possibilities of myself beyond this world and the stars
I sing the joy of wandering and the pleasure of a wanderer's death)

Since every line contains at least one pronoun referring to Apollinaire, this is clearly an important personal statement. The second stanza, which is largely a restatement of the first, has one purpose: to present Apollinaire's poetic credo. This is the major theme of both stanzas, whose function is to justify "Le Musicien de Saint-Merry" and the poet's work in general. Apollinaire's *ars poetica*, summarized in lines 1 and 6, is simply this: he asserts the primacy of pure, unrestricted imagination in poetry, unfettered by the demands of reality.[19] Lines 1, 3, and 5 emphasize the fantastic nature of his story, and lines 2 and 7 anticipate the story itself. The last line, in which "errer" has the double meaning of "to wander" and "to be mistaken," also asserts Apollinaire's right to experiment, even at the risk of failure. In the last analysis, then, the song Apollinaire is singing is the poem itself. The act of singing corresponds to the act of poetic creation. And if the faceless musician is playing Apollinaire's "song," that is, composing the poem, he must be identical to Apollinaire. More precisely, he is a fantasized version of the author—Apollinaire as he wished to see himself. For he possesses one key attribute not found in the author of "La Chanson du Mal-Aimé": irresistible attractiveness to women.

Insofar as the faceless protagonist represents Apollinaire the poet, it is appropriate that at least five of his female followers are taken directly from his works.[20] One of them—Mia—also seems to have been a former love of his in Monaco. The fact that the women are prostitutes is as important as their rapturous subservience. For if Apollinaire suffered mightily at the hands of his various loves (and his mother), he was finally able to punish them in this poem as he could never do in real life. In his misogynistic mood, he lumps all women together under the heading "prostitute" and disposes of them as he wishes. As one critic states, "le poète s'installe en quelque sorte comme le spectateur de son propre triomphe—que ce triomphe soit sur les femmes nommées, sur toutes les femmes du monde, ou sur l'amour lui-même" ("The poet installs himself in a way as the spectator of his own triumph—whether this triumph is over the women he names, over all the women in the world, or over love itself").[21] Apollinaire's revenge assumes two forms. In one, which belongs to the mythic dimension of the poem, he leads the women to Hades/Hell. The theme of death runs through the entire poem, and one has seen that the women enter the abandoned house "without regretting what they had left behind . . . light, *life*, or memory") (vv. 84–86, emphasis added). Renaud believes that the faceless Apollinaire disappears along with them, symbolizing a break with the past, but this does not seem to be true. For one thing, he is characterized as a "ferryman of the dead" (v. 9), transporting his charges to the underworld but not remaining there himself. For another, in the dramatic version of the poem (see Chap. 3) he reappears on stage at the end.

The other form of revenge is erotic: Apollinaire takes the women for himself, consigning them to his own personal harem. It should be stressed that the faceless musician is not indifferent to his followers, as some critics have charged, but merely *unconcerned;* ("indifférent," v. 30, having both meanings). He simply has complete confidence in his power over the women (as well he should), and it is this power that makes him so "terrible" (v. 31). In fact, he is described as "heureux" (v. 56), that is, both happy and fortunate. The nature of his happiness—and the destination of the women—are evident from the erotic epithet that is applied to him: he is a "melodious ravisher" (v. 29). Finally, without going into details at this point, it appears that the mysterious "man with no eyes no nose and no ears" is actually a *membrum virile* (Apollinaire's).22 In its erect state it is eminently worthy of the prostitutes' attention. Thus sexual fantasy and revenge blend in an image of irresistable phallic magnetism.23

Like Apollinaire's revenge, the occasional touches of melancholy are motivated by the recent demise of his relationship with Marie Laurencin, traces of which are scattered throughout the poem. For example he invokes their mutual suffering following the breakup in the lines: "But we who are dying because we live too far apart / Stretch out our arms . . ." (vv. 46–47). His longing for reconciliation is exposed here like a bare nerve. These lines are also the key to understanding the puzzling statement: "And now / You resemble me unhappily you resemble me" (vv. 49–50), which recalls Baudelaire's ""Hypocrite lecteur,—mon semblable,—mon frère!" ("Hypocrite reader—my fellow human being—my brother") in the Introduction to *Les Fleurs du mal.* Addressing Marie, Apollinaire detects an ironic resemblance, which he expresses via a *jeu de mots* centered on "malheureusement." On the one hand they are both "unfortunate"; on the other they resemble each other because they are "unhappy." This emotional state contrasts sharply with that of the "happy musician." As Poupon has shown, the line "Seated next to me you were crying in the back of a horse-drawn cab" (v. 48) recalls how Apollinaire had recently consoled Marie upon the death of her mother. The line "She crosses a bridge connecting Bonn and Beuel and disappears in the direction of Pützchen" (v. 39) probably also refers to Marie—with echoes of Annie Playden. For this is the path followed by Tristouse Ballerinette, Marie's double, in *Le Poète assassiné*.[24]

Despite their fragmentary appearance, the preceding lines are not gratuitous. The references to Marie are separated and isolated on the page to indicate that they are random thoughts and memories passing through Apollinaire's mind. They also serve to prepare the conclusion, where the different themes are finally resolved:

> Voici le soir
> A Saint-Merry c'est l'Angélus qui sonne
> Cortèges ô cortèges
> C'est quand jadis le roi revenait de Vincennes
> Il vint une troupe de casquettiers
> Il vint des marchands de bananes
> Il vint des soldats de la garde républicaine
> O nuit
> Troupeau de regards langoureux des femmes
> O nuit
> Toi ma douleur et mon attente vaine
> J'entends mourir le son d'une flûte lointaine
>
> (It is evening
> At Saint-Merry the Angelus is ringing
> Processions oh processions
> When long ago the king would return from Vincennes
> There came a troop of hatters
> There came some banana pedlars
> There came some Republican Guardsmen
> Oh night
> Flock of langurous feminine glances
> Oh night
> You my sorrow and my vain expectation
> I hear the sound of a flute dying away in the distance)

There is a distinct break with the preceding story, paralleling the coming of night. Like the daylight, the main event is finished, and the ringing of the Angelus serves as the line of demarcation between fantasy and reality. Recalling another confrontation with the supernatural, that is, the Anunciation, the Angelus seems rather ironic. For if it commemorates "le Salut que l'Ange prédit" ("the Salvation predicted by the Angel," Villon, *Le Lais*), salvation seems extremely remote for the women in the poem who have been led off to eternal damnation.

More importantly, the bells mark the hour of evening prayer, calling to mind Millet's painting *L'Angélus* and its atmosphere of utter tranquility.[25] Once the flurry of activity has ceased, a similar peace descends on the Saint-Merry quarter, where one sees Apollinaire the poet left alone with his memories in a setting full of historical memories. The line "Flock of languorous feminine glances," which may be a metaphor for the sky filled with stars (cf. "Voyage"), represents the memory of the women in his life as well as those in the poem. Apollinaire's anguish ("douleur") stems from his isolation. Just as he is alone in the Saint-Merry streets, he is alone in life. His immediate source of anguish is the loss of Marie, the "you" of the next-to-last line. While he had initially hoped for a reconciliation (v. 4), his expectations have proved to be in vain (v. 101). The contrast is striking: surrounded by women who throng to become the slaves of the musician, Apollinaire himself has been unable to capture the woman he loves. The last verb, *mourir* ("to die"), underlines the finality of his failure. In the last analysis his anguish is an avowal of his impotence. The final line, with its blending of memory, music, and love's suffering, recalls the ending of "Cors de chasse." In both poems the music fading in the distance symbolizes the passage of life itself.

The Pied Piper of Hamelin

Wishing to give "Le Musicien de Saint-Merry" a mythic dimension that would surpass his personal experience, Apollinaire first chose to graft the legend of the Pied Piper of Hamelin onto his initial guided-tour structure. This idea may have been suggested by the statue of a piper on the main facade of the Eglise de Saint-Merry or by a guidebook note that the rue Saint-Martin was inhabited by musicians and *jongleurs* in the Middle Ages.[26] The salient features of the legend, which exists in several versions, are the following: on either 26 June or 22 July 1284, having been refused payment for ridding Hamelin of its rats, a mysterious piper took his revenge by piping away 130 children and disappearing with them into a cavern high on Koppenberg Hill. In some versions the mountain opens up to swallow them instead.[27] The last sound anyone hears is that of flute music gradually dying away. The disappearance is commemorated first by a painting on the church window and secondly by a column bearing the names of the children. From this brief outline it is clear that the influence of the legend was crucial. The precise date, the flute-player with his irresistable music, the theme of revenge, the disappearance by engulfment, the fading flute music at the end—all these are repeated in "Le Musicien de Saint-Merry," whose shape they largely determine.

Which version of the tale Apollinaire drew on is impossible to say. There is nothing about Mérimée's account—singled out by Poupon—that particularly qualifies it for this honor. The intriguing possibility exists that Apollinaire may have been influenced by Goethe, whom he admired, and whose poem "Der Rattenfänger" metamorphoses the rat-catcher into a woman-catcher in the last stanza:

>Dann ist der vielgewandte Sänger
>Gelegentlich ein Mädchenfänger,
>In keinem Städtchen langt er an,
>Wo er's nicht mancher angetan.
>Und wären Mädchen noch so blöde,
>Und wären Weiber noch so spröde:
>Doch allen wird so liebebang
>Bei Zaubersaiten and Gesang.

>(Sometimes the wandering singer
>Becomes a maiden-catcher.
>There is no village in which
>He does not cause many to fall in love with him.
>And however bashful the maidens may be,
>And however coy the women,
>They are all rendered amorous
>By his magic strings and song.)

Goethe's rat-catcher is not a flute-player, however. He sings and accompanies himself on a lute, and as such resembles a wandering minstrel more than the Pied Piper.

The Prostitutes' Procession

Apollinaire skilfully integrated *cortèges* on another three levels that dovetail perfectly with the Hamelin legend. As noted, the different versions specify either 26 June or 22 July as the day of the *exodus hamelensis*. These are the saint's days of John and Paul on the one hand, and of Mary Magdelene on the other. In his treatise *Des divinités génératrices chez les anciens et les modernes* (which

Apollinaire owned) J. A. Dulaure devotes some interesting pages to prostitution in medieval Paris, including the Saint-Merry quarter. He states, for example, that the prostitutes belonged to a special guild with its own rules, judges, and taxes, and that once every year they filed across Paris in a solemn procession. This day was, appropriately, Mary Magdalene's Day.[28] There is little doubt that "Le Musicien de Saint-Merry" incorporates this historical procession, which parallels the theme of modern-day prostitutes pursuing potential customers in the same area. While the role of this procession is minor, it links the protagonist's followers to the mythic figure of Mary Magdalene (the Eternal Whore)—whose first name in French is also Marie. Similarly, if we do not know which Pied Piper account Apollinaire used, we know it was a version with the 22 July date.

The Devil

On yet another level the critics are unanimous in interpreting Apollinaire's faceless musician as a manifestation of the Devil. In this context it is noteworthy that the Pied Piper legend has a definite demonic aspect and that the Piper is identified with the Devil in disguise in many versions.[29] In the legend, as in the poem, the hypnotic flute music represents a form of sorcery. Apollinaire may also have been inspired by a statue on the main facade of the Église de Saint-Merry replacing a religious figure destroyed during the Revolution. One guidebook states: "Another blunder of the modern architect is the placing of a demon on the center—at the point of the arch, where the Medieval artists invariably put the figure of Christ or Our Lady."[30] From this it is easy to imagine a church devoted to the worship of Satan, and indeed Poupon reports that "toute une tradition occultiste situe l'enfer sous l'église Saint-Merry, église suspecte où des rites démoniaques se seraient déroulés" ("There is a whole occult tradition that situates Hell beneath the Saint-Merry church, a suspicious church in which demonic rites are supposed to have taken place"). Unfortunately, he offers no documentation. In any event the demonic component of the faceless musician is acknowledged at the beginning of the poem:

> Passeur des morts et les mordannantes mériennes
> Des millions de mouches éventaient une splendeur

>   (Ferryman of the dead and swarming Merry-widows
>   Millions of flies were fanning a splendor)
>
> (vv. 9–10)

The key to these verses lies in the image of the flies. Poupon takes the second line as a metaphor for the moon and the stars. Here, as elsewhere in his works, Apollinaire evokes the image of infernal flies, who, being female, are associated with dancing and eroticism. Moreover, as the symbols of death and putrefaction, they are inextricably bound up with Beelzebub, Lord of the Flies.[31] In "Le Musicien de Saint-Merry" they not only serve to identify the protagonist but foreshadow the end of the poem where the women are led off to death/Hell. As in "Voyage," Apollinaire is in effect wishing that his former loves—that all women—would go to the Devil.

The two lines above, which announce the appearance of the protagonist in the next line, prefigure the procession of the musician and his women. Their relation to one another is chiasmic. "Ferryman of the dead" and "splendor" describe Beelzebub, while the "swarming Merry-widows" and "millions of flies" are his female followers. The flies are metaphors for the prostitutes (and vice versa), who are attracted to the unclean in swarms and who are unclean themselves. This metaphorical metamorphosis is likewise evident in the epithet *mordonnantes,* a portmanteau word but also a pun. For if it combines *mort* ("death") and *donnant* ("dealing"), it just as obviously fuses *mordant* ("biting") and *bourdonnant* ("buzzing").[32] On the one hand the "mériennes" are seen as death-dealing women companions, even accomplices, of the ferryman. On the other, they are depicted as a swarm of biting, buzzing (cf. the verb *éventer,* "to fan") flies. As prostitutes, they are lethal in the first instance and annoying in the second. The two images are inextricably intertwined, leaving the reader with the image of hordes of whores-flies performing an obscene *danse funèbre*.

The Myth of Dionysos

Within the realm of ancient Greek mythology Apollinaire's hero has been identified as Hermes (Boisson), Orpheus (Renaud, Richter, Bates, Paz), Pan (Bates), and Dionysos (Bates). Detailed investigation fails to substantiate the first three claims, but the fourth has much to recommend it. This is not to deny that

Apollinaire's works are full of references to Hermes, Orpheus, and Pan, or that these figures are sometimes associated with groups of women, or that his first collection of poetry was subtitled *Cortège d'Orphée*. However, none of their legends make sense in the context of the poem. If Orpheus's music had the power to charm wild animals, his instrument was the lyre, not the flute. It is symptomatic that Renaud is compelled to postulate "une sorte d'Anti-Orphée, d'Orphée retourné" ("a sort of Anti-Orpheus, an upside-down Orpheus") to explain why Orpheus seems to be leading Eurydice down to Hades instead of rescuing her.[33] Similarly, if Pan usually played "musique pastorale" like Apollinaire's musician (v. 72), his instrument was not the flute but the pan-pipe (syrinx). Neither are his association with fright and bestiality helpful. As Scott Bates notes, it is *Dionysos*—a flute-player—who is associated with Ariadne (Ariane).[34] Abandoned on the isle of Naxos by Theseus, Ariadne was subsequently rescued by Dionysos and became his consort. The story of the encounter and rescue was popularized in 1912 by Richard Strauss's opera *Adriane auf Naxos*. It is tempting to connect Apollinaire's Ariadne with Daedalus's labyrinth and the story of the thread, as several critics have done, but like Strauss, Apollinaire seems to refer only to her post-Thesean history. While the Saint-Merry quarter is indeed labyrinthine, the procession itself is uncomplicated, and Ariadne is a follower not a leader.

It is possible that Apollinaire combined the Dionysos myth and the Pied Piper story on his own initiative. However an intriguing precedent exists in the writings of Nietzsche, who seems to have influenced the dramatic version of "Le Musicien de Saint-Merry" via Giorgio de Chirico. This influence may well extend back to the original poem. The passage in question occurs in *Jenseits von Gut und Böse (Beyond Good and Evil)*:

> Das genie des Herzens, wie es jener grosse Verborgene hat, der Versucher-Gott und geborene Rattenfänger der Gewissen, dessen Stimme bis in die Unterwelt jeder Seele hinabzusteigen weiss, welcher nicht ein Wort sagt, nicht ein Blick blickt, indem nicht eine Rücksicht und Falte der Lockung läge, zu dessen Meisterschaft es gehört, dass er zu scheinen versteht—und nicht das, was er ist, sondern was denen, die ihm folgen, ein Zwang mehr ist, um sich immer näher an ihn zu drängen, um ihn immer innerlicher und gründlicher zu folgen.

> (The genius of the heart, as that great mysterious one possesses it, the tempter-god and born rat-catcher of consciences, whose voice can

descend into the underworld of every soul, who neither speaks a word nor casts a glance which is lacking in allurement, to whose perfection it seems that he knows how to appear—not as he is, but in a guise which acts as an additional constraint on his followers to press ever closer to him, to follow him more cordially and thoroughly.[35]

Nietzsche eventually identifies his mysterious personage as "der Gott Dionysos, jener grosse Zweideutige und Versucher-Gott" ("the god Dionysos, that great equivocator and tempter") and pairs him with Ariadne. The parallels with "Le Musicien de Saint-Merry" are striking. First, Nietzsche's protagonist is simultaneously Dionysos and the Pied Piper of Hamelin ("geborene Rattenfänger"). Secondly, his irresistable personal magnetism—enhanced by a disguise—attracts hordes of followers. And thirdly, he is connected with a descent into the underworld. These parellels are so marked that they can scarcely be concidental.

It is evident, in any case, that Apollinaire's poem reproduces part of the Dionysos myth. In the latter Dionysos wanders about the East (cf. Apollinaire's "I sing the joy of wandering") playing his flute and accompanied by a band of *maenades*, ecstatic female followers crowned with vine leaves and carrying the thyrsus. There is an even greater resemblance to Euripides' *Bacchae*, in which Dionysos enchants the entire female population of Thebes who abandon their homes to go off with him. Not for nothing do the *Homeric Hymns* call him the "inspirer of frenzied women." In *The Bacchae*, as in Apollinaire's poem, the motive behind the abduction/seduction is one of revenge. Moreover, the death of Pentheus at the end parallels the disappearance of the "mériennes," both of which may be seen as sacrifices to Dionysos. In this context it is tempting to view the biting, buzzing flies as modern-day Eumenides or Furies (cf. Sartre's *Les Mouches*).

The Phallic Procession

If "Le Musicien de Saint-Merry" incorporates the Dionysos myth, it also refers to the *worship* of Dionysos, that is, to specific religious ceremonies. Apollinaire superimposes the structure of an actual Dionysian rite upon his Pied Piper framework—the phallic procession. As noted previously, the physical source of the musician is clearly anatomical. Representing the *membrum virile*, the faceless man is "dark with a strawberry blush on his cheeks" and is devoid of any physiognomy except for a mouth—a description which accords with the facts. One should thus imagine him as a human body surmounted by a smooth, spherical head. As numerous classicists have noted, the phallus was the symbol *par excellence* of Dionysos and figured prominently in seasonal processions honoring the god.[36] According to one authority, "la procession avait probablement caractère d'un charme destiné à promouvoir la fertilité des champs et des jardins et la fécondité des foyers" ("the procession was probably a sort of spell destined to promote the fertility of the fields and gardens and the fecundity of the home"[37] The joyous mood and bawdy songs of these ceremonial festivities can be glimpsed in Aristophanes' *Acharnians*, which Apollinaire certainly knew, and in the *History* of Herodotus (2. 48). The typical procession was headed by one or more flute-players, followed by several maidens (*canephoroi*) carrying baskets on their heads with materials for sacrifice. Then came the *phallophoroi*, bearing an enormous phallus, followed by a chorus of musicians and the *ithyphalloi*, men dressed in women's clothing, pretending drunkenness and singing phallic songs. The procession culminated in a sacrifice of cakes and porridge. Dulaure, who describes the Dionysian procession in detail, remarks concerning the costume of the *phallophoroi:* "C'étaient des hommes qui ne portaient point de masque sur leur visage, mais qui le couvraient avec un tissu formé par des feuilles de lierre, de serpolet et d'acanthe" ("These men did not wear masks but covered their faces with a fabric made from ivy, thyme, and acanthus leaves").[38] Thus the phallus-bearers represented phalli themselves, and as men "with no eyes no nose and no ears" they prefigure Apollinaire's phallomorphic hero to an astonishing degree. The poet clearly integrated the key elements of the procession (flute, phallus, *phallophoroi*, female followers) into his poem.[39] The giant Dionysian phallus and its bearers inspired the physical appearance of his protagonist, while the worship of the phallus as a fertility symbol suggested the worship of the phallus *as phallus*. This concept dovetails perfectly with his sexual fantasies and their representation in the poem.

The Sexual Cosmology

The existence in "Le Musicien de Saint-Merry" of another level, whose scope surpasses that of myth and ritual, has been implicit in much of the preceding discussion. For insofar as mythic characters and actions lend themselves to symbolic interpretation, they belong to a larger pattern—that governing life itself. As such, they exemplify universal principles and dramatize the human condition. One indication that Apollinaire wishes readers to consider his poem in this perspective concerns the faceless musician: "He was playing the flute and the music guided his steps" (v. 15). This is an astonishing bit of information: the musician is not a free agent. Like his female followers he must follow the path indicated by his music. This means that he is not the creator of the music he is playing but rather its vehicle. Alternately "charmeur et charmé" ("enchanter and enchanted"—Poupon), he is moved by the same irresistable force as the women and is subject to some greater power (symbolized by the music). If at one level this represents poetic inspiration, here it represents the life force itself that Apollinaire associates with sexuality. In directing their steps according to the imperious commands of the music, the faceless man and his troupe are performing the dance of life—which in several respects resembles the dance of the flies about the "splendeur." Both are situated within the confines of birth and death; both are automatic responses to instinctual impulses.

In shifting from the Pied Piper to Dionysos, from demon to *daimon*, Apollinaire chose the perfect vehicle for his sexual life force. As a fertility god, Dionysos's significance far surpassed his importance as an individual. According to one authority, "[il]réunit en sa personne le représentant du monde infernal et le daïmôn en qui et par qui l'exubérance de la nature éclate dans la floraison du printemps et dans la fructifération de l'automne" (["He] was both the representative of the underworld and the spirit in which and by which nature's exuberance is expressed in the flowering of spring and the fructification of autumn").[40] As such, he was involved with the interplay of sexual forces in nature and with the concept of potency or sexual power. In the Greek cosmology, which resembled Apollinaire's, birth and death were interpreted in terms of sexuality. The death of vegetation in the fall was attributed to a loss of potency (symbolized by Dionysos's descent into the underworld), and its (re)birth in the spring resulted from an increase in potency (the ascent of Dionysos). If one substitutes "fertility" for "potency," the same concept applies to Ariadne, who became the consort of Dionysos precisely because she was already a fertility goddess. Thus the Greek cosmology was dualistic and divided the world into male and female.

"Le Musicien de Saint-Merry" is informed by an identical worldview. Scholars have observed that Apollinaire's poetry is shaped by a dialectic of opposites, corresponding to the functioning of the psyche itself according to Freud. Thus fire is opposed to water, death to rebirth, past to future, and so forth.⁴¹ In the present poem the dialectic is primarily sexual. Paralleling the biological separation of the sexes, the world is divided into masculine and feminine, active and passive, *animus* and *anima*. Apollinaire evokes this dichotomy at the beginning, interrupting the description of his protagonist with the following apostrophe:

>   Man Oh! Ariadne
>   (v. 14)

Although the male/female opposition is anticipated by the pairing of the ferryman with the Merry-widows in line 9, the entrance of Dionysos and Ariadne here officially announces the theme. The dichotomy is structural as well as thematic, for it extends throughout the poem and polarizes the various processions into opposing sexual camps. It is evident in the following couples: the musician and his women, Apollinaire and Marie, the prostitutes and their customers, the phallus and the *canephoroi*, Beelzebub and the female flies, the Devil and Mary Magdalene. Moreover, the poem is sprinkled with sexual symbols. Among the masculine symbols are the magic flute, the industrial smokestacks, the bananas, and the flautist himself in his phallic costume. The feminine symbols include the fountain, the various women, the open door, the broken windows, and the empty house that finally engulfs the procession. The Apollinarian universe is thus a highly sexualized entity, reflecting his belief tht "la sexualité est l'élément prépondérant dans la vie humaine" ("sexuality is the primary element in human life").⁴²

Despite its sexual polarization, however, Apollinaire's universe is not the least bit fragmentary. If male and female exist as separate, distinct entities, they are not totally self-contained. Nor are they hopelessly isolated. Each category is meaningful only in the context of the other. It is the tension between them that generates the sexual life force—a sort of electric current passing between the positive and negative poles of the universe. Thus Eros is the connecting link between male and female, between man and woman. Eros holds the universe together and provides its motive force. Apollinaire clearly had this function in mind when he spoke in one place of "L'amour qui emplit ainsi que la lumière / Tout le solide espace entre les étoiles et les planètes" ("Love that fills like light / All the solid space between the stars and the planets") ("Poème lu au mariage d'André Salmon"). Even more revealing is his pronouncement elsewhere that "l'amour guide toute la nature" ("love guides all of nature"). Postulated as a universal law governing the categories of animal, vegetable, and mineral, this statement summarizes the worldview underlying "Le Musicien de Saint-Merry"[43]

Throughout the foregoing analysis the one constant, recurring theme has been sexuality in its various forms—from commercial commodity to the basis of love to universal principle. Each of the parallel narrative structures represents the projection of primal desire at a distinct level of meaning, ranging from autobiographical concerns to mythic preoccupations. For, as André Breton points out, "la région où s'érige le désir sans contrainte . . . est aussi celle où les mythes prennent leur essor" ("the region where boundless desire exists . . . is also that where myths take wing").[44] The eventual integration of the various dimensions takes place at the level of the work of art itself. To insist on a single theme, however, is to ignore the poem's complexity. As one uncovers successive layers of meaning, one comes to realize that its subject is really *life*. This explains why Apollinaire's personal experiences (past and present) are juxtaposed with life in general (actual and historical). Conceived initially as a fantasy of revenge enacted against a backdrop of desire, the poem goes beyond its original premises to dramatize the structures of human existence.

3
A Train Leaves for Paris

In July 1914 Apollinaire created an intriguing pantomime in collaboration with three other individuals—two artists and a musician. Entitled *A quelle heure un train partira-t-il pour Paris? (What Time Does a Train Leave for Paris?)*, the authoritative manuscript was discovered a few years ago in a private library in the United States.[1] The title, which seems enigmatic at first, refers to "Le Musicien de Saint-Merry" (v. 33) where the poet evokes a conversation taking place in a provincial railroad station. Consisting of a script by Apollinaire, "music by Alberto Savinio, scenery and costumes by Francis Picabia and Marius de Zayas," the pantomime was modeled on the earlier poem. One of the strangest examples of international artistic collaboration in the twentieth century, it was the product of a French poet born in Rome but whose nationality was Russian; an Italian born in Greece; a painter born in Paris of a French mother and a Cuban father, and a Mexican caricaturist belonging to the New York avant-garde. Among the various forces converging on this work are Symbolism, Cubism, Futurism, simultanism, Dada, Surrealism, abstract art, and Metaphysical painting. Unfortunately the music and drawings for this production, if they ever existed, seem to have disappeared. In any case the outbreak of World War I in August prevented the collaborators from carrying out their project, whose revolutionary aspect would have electrified the avant-garde.

Marius de Zayas

Before examining *A quelle heure*, a brief history of the relations among the four collaborators will establish some necessary points of reference. Marius de Zayas (fig. 2), a caricaturist and writer of Mexican origin, had been a member of the New York avant-garde since 1907.[2] Closely associated with Alfred Stieglitz in particular,

NEW-YORK

Intéressante conférence de M. de Zayas, au *Columbia*, sur l'humour yankee. Cette conférence, première du genre, fut sans paroles et singulièrement démonstrative, néanmoins. Nous sommes autorisés à en publier l'approximatif schéma.

La scène représente une promenade publique. Ormes et banc.
Un matelot, qu'accompagne un mannequin exactement semblable à lui-même, entre par le côté cour et vient prendre place sur le banc. Homme et mannequin portent sous le bras droit le national béret bleu à rayures concentriques blanches. Après quelques instants de réflexion profonde, le matelot se lève et sort par le côté jardin, abandonnant son compagnon extatique. Un monsieur passe qui, prenant pour cible le national béret bleu à rayures concentriques blanches, tire un coup de revolver. Le compagnon extatique ne bronche pas, cependant que le gentleman nerveux le crible de balles. Le monsieur sort enfin par le côté jardin et le matelot rentre par le côté cour. Le compagnon extatique disparaît dans les frises. Le matelot s'assied et le gentleman revient, accompagné d'une dame. — Prenant pour cible le national béret bleu a rayures blanches concentriques, il vise et va faire feu. Mais le matelot se lève. Swing et direct, crochet à la mâchoire. Le monsieur tombe et la dame s'évanouit. Le matelot sort en esquissant une petite gigue.

Rideau.

La solennité prit fin sur une lumineuse présentation, par M. de Zayas lui-même, du dernier état de la caricature politique. Un admirable masque canaque fut apporté. Et M. de Zayas l'adorna de moustaches dites *en crocs*.

2. Francis Picabia, *Marius de Zayas*. Ink drawing. From *391*, March 1, 1917.

he contributed to the latter's *Camera work* and exhibited at the famous "291" gallery on Fifth Avenue. In 1910 and 1911 he spent an entire year in Paris, where he developed an enthusiasm for modern art. De Zayas was especially impressed by Picasso, who lent eighty-three works for an exhibition at "291," and the two men quickly became good friends. In 1913 he published *A Study of the Modern Evolution of Plastic Form* (co-authored by Paul B. Haviland), one of the earliest American attempts to understand modern art. On 13 May 1914 de Zayas returned to Paris with the intention of obtaining works for "291" and of making caricatures of various celebrities.[3] He was welcomed by Francis Picabia who, in gratitude for de Zayas's hospitality the previous year during the Armory Show in New York, helped him to carry out his project. Picabia also introduced him to Apollinaire and the group associated with his review *Les Soirées de Paris*. On 25 May Apollinaire reported his arrival in *Paris-Journal:*

> M. de Zayas, qui a renouvelé avec un talent extraordinaire l'art de la caricature et qui a introduit en Amérique Picasso et Picabia . . . se trouve en ce moment à Paris, dans le but de faire la caricature des hommes les plus nouveaux de tous les arts, la littérature et la musique.
>
> (M. de Zayas, who has renewed the art of caricature with extraordinary talent and who introduced Picasso and Picabia to America . . . is presently in Paris. He intends to make caricatures of the most advanced individuals in the arts, in literature, and in music.)[4]

De Zayas's correspondence with Stieglitz reveals that he and the French poet hit it off immediately and arranged to exchange their respective journals (including back issues). Although Apollinaire and his friends were not entirely unknown in New York, it was de Zayas who finally effected a meaningful rapprochement between the two groups. On 3 June 1914 Stieglitz responded: "That the *Soirées de Paris* crowd must be interesting goes without saying. [Paul B.] Haviland, you know, gets its magazine. And I have heard about it from other sources." On 9 June following de Zayas's suggestion, Stieglitz wrote that he was sending several copies of *Camera Work*, which he hoped would go to "the right people."

> Above all I will be only too glad to know Apollinaire gets it. I would have sent copies to him long ago, but I did not want to make it look as if we wanted to get something out of him. . . . But now that you have brought about the connection between "291" and that little "crowd," we are not so apt to be misunderstood.

3. Marius de Zayas, *Guillaume Apollinaire*. Ink drawing. From *Les Soirées de Paris,* July–August 1914.

4. Marius de Zayas, *Francis Picabia*. Ink drawing. From *Les Soirées de Paris*, July–August 1914.

Most of June, however, was spent on assignment in London making caricatures of important writers. Returning to Paris toward the end of the month, de Zayas wrote Stieglitz:

> The last word in Paris is the "Simultanism" in literature. Apollinaire is the father of it. I recommend you to read in the last number of the *Soirées* his "Carte-Océan" ["Lettre-Océan"]. It is really very amusing. This Apollinaire is really the deepest observer of superficiality. We have become good friends.

One week later Apollinaire devoted his entire art column in *Paris-Journal* to an enthusiastic review of de Zayas's caricatures, repeatedly expressing his admiration for the artist and his drawings, which, in his opinion, were "d'accord avec l'art des peintres contemporains les plus audacieux" ("in keeping with the art of the boldest contemporary painters").[5] In a letter to Stieglitz the next day (9 July) de Zayas wrote:

> I am working hard in making these people understand the convenience of a commerce of ideas with America. And I want to absorb the spirit of what they are doing to bring it to "291." We need a closer contact with Paris, there is no question about it. The *Soirées de Paris* is going to publish four of my caricatures in the next number: Vollard's Apollinaire's, Picabia's, and yours.

As announced, the caricatures (figs. 3 and 4) appeared in the July–August issue of *Les Soirées de Paris*, where their forceful abstraction attracted favorable comments. Elsewhere in the same letter de Zayas proposed a publishing project and discussed Apollinaire's experiments with visual poetry:

> I have gotten from Apollinaire a series of articles he published on Rousseau with many of his letters. If they interest you and [you] want to publish them in a booklet (they make only about 80 pages), he will be able to get about 24 photographs of his best paintings. I also have gotten from him some of the originals of his new poems which are creating among the crowd of modernists a real sensation. He is doing in poetry what Picasso is doing in painting. He uses actual forms made up with letters. All these show a tendency towards the fusion of the so-called arts. I am sure that this mode of expression will interest you.

The outbreak of World War I three weeks later put an end to the projected booklet on the Douanier Rousseau. The correspondence reveals that a Rousseau exhibition at "291" was also in the works, with paintings to be lent by "a Russian girl," but that these had to be left behind when de Zayas finally sailed for America. He did manage to bring back a collection of African sculpture borrowed from the art dealer Paul Guillaume. In any case it is interesting that de Zayas chose to associate Apollinaire's visual poetry with Picasso rather than with the Futurists, whose works more nearly resembled his experiments with the *calligramme*. One wonders if de Zayas might have been repeating something he heard Apollinaire say. In addition the original poems that he mentioned have recently come to light. Apollinaire gave each of the collaborators on *A quelle heure* a set of manuscripts for a different calligram. De Zayas received those for "Paysage," Savinio those for "Lettre-Océan," and Picabia those for "Coeur couronne et mirroir."[6] In his letter of 9 July de Zayas wrote that he planned to return to London the following week and to leave for New York 1 August. Whether he actually went to England is unknown, for the correspondence breaks off at this point. If so, he was back in Paris by 19 July with an ambitious project. In a brief note Apollinaire reported in *Paris-Journal* that "le caricaturiste le plus moderne, Marius de Zayas, se propose d'écrire un essai sur 'l'évolution de la forme à travers les âges' " ("Marius de Zayas, the most modern of caricaturists, plans to write an essay on 'The Evolution of Form through the Ages' ").[7] On 12 September, one month later than he had anticipated, de Zayas finally managed to return to New York.[8]

Alberto Savinio

Like Marius de Zayas, Alberto Savinio (fig. 5) deserves to be much better known. Fortunately, after sixty years of neglect, he is finally beginning to receive some critical attention.[9] A talented musician, composer, poet, painter, novelist, dramatist, translator, and short-story writer, Savinio was a veritable *uomo universale*. Despite his considerable talent, however, he has remained in the shadow of his brother, Giorgio de Chirico. Born in Athens, where he continued to live until the age of thirteen, he was baptized Andrea de Chirico. After living in Italy and in Germany, where he studied under the composer and organist Max Reger, Savinio arrived in Paris early in 1911 with his mother and brother. Between 1911 and 1914 little is known of his occupations, although he seems to have composed several musical works. Since Apollinaire appears to have met his brother sometime during

5. Giorgio de Chirico, *Portrait of His Brother Andrea*, 1910. Oil on canvas, 47 × 29-1/2″. Collection Nationalgalerie, Staatliche Museen zu Berlin.

1912, he probably became acquainted with Savinio during the same period. Not until 1914, however, did he join Apollinaire's inner circle of friends. Interestingly this event coincided with Savinio's conversion to the modern movement, that was publicized in *Les Soirées de Paris* and elsewhere.

One first picks up Savinio's trail in the 15 April issue of *Les Soirées de Paris,* which featured a long article by him entitled "Le Drame et la musique." This article, which will be considered in chapter 4, described his new aesthetic in detail and proposed a new relationship between drama and music. The following month Savinio was very much in evidence. Among other things, the entire first page of *Les Soirées de Paris* was devoted to an announcement of a recital by Savinio on Sunday, 24 May, in the journal's offices. Consisting of ten selections from four different works, it was to include the following compositions: dances from *Le Trésor de Rampsénit, Deux Amours dans la nuit, Persée,* and *Niobé (The Treasure of Rampsénit, Two Loves in the Night, Perseus,* and *Niobé).* The first was an *opéra bouffe* by M. D. Calvocoressi, the second a ballet by Calvocoressi and Savinio, the third, a ballet by Michel Fokine for the Ballets Russes, and the last a ballet-drama by Calvocoressi. The latter was a prominent music critic and an old family friend of the de Chiricos from Athens. The following page contained a lengthy note in which Savinio discussed his work in general and his approaching recital. Of his four compositions, he explained, only the last one—*Niobé*—conformed to the criteria established in his April article. Even though the music for *Deux Amours dans la nuit* and *Persée* had been composed fairly recently, it represented his former, traditional style. In his opinion only *Niobé* could be considered truly modern.

On 24 May, the day of the concert, Apollinaire devoted a long column in *Paris-Journal* to Savinio in which he sought to publicize the recital and to acquaint the public with the composer's music. One part of the article was concerned with Savinio's musical theories. Another part emphasized his forceful style and his extreme modernity:

> Les privilégiés qui auront l'honneur d'assister à ce premier concert de musique nouvelle seront étonnés de la brutalité avec laquelle le jeune musicien traite son instrument.
> Elle est un témoignage de l'énergie qui anime notre artiste.
> On le verra touchant son piano. Il s'y tient en bras de chemise, monocle à l'oeil, se démène, hurle tandis que l'instrument fait ce qu'il peut pour atteindre au diapason enthousiaste du musicien.

(Those privileged to attend this first concert devoted to new music will be astonished at the brutality with which the young musician treats his instrument.)

This is a symptom of the artist's energy.

One will see him playing the piano in his shirt sleeves, a monocle in his eye, throwing himself about, shouting while the instrument does its best to attain the musician's enthusiastic range.)[10]

Elsewhere Apollinaire included a list of the works to be performed and added one not mentioned previously: *Les Chants de la mi-mort (Songs of Living Death)*, based on a series of dramatic poems by Savinio himself.

Apollinaire's column of 1 June in the *Mercure de France* contained a review of Savinio's recital on 24 May in which he stressed the musician's power and energy.[11] Borrowing the pseudonym Jean Cérusse from his co-editors of *Les Soirées de Paris*, who were on vacation, he also published a laudatory review in the June issue of that magazine. On 7 July, writing in *Paris-Journal,* he reported that the young composer had attended the newspaper's weekly dinner, where he performed his music and drew some remarkable caricatures of the diners. He added that Albert Savinio "se rend à Londres, où M. Serge de Diaghilew l'invite pour y traiter de l'acquisition de la musique d'importants ouvrages chorégraphiques, dont l'un, *Persée*, fut spécialment composé et commandé à Savinio par M. Michel Fokine, le remarquable metteur en scène des ballets russes" (Albert Savinio "is leaving for London, where M. Serge de Diaghilew has invited him to discuss the possibility of commissioning music for some important ballets—one of which, *Perseus*, was commissioned and composed at the request of M. Michel Fokine, the remarkable directeur of the Russian Ballet").[12] On 15 July Apollinaire published a second pseudonymous article in *Les Soirées de Paris*. Entitled "Albert Savinio et la nouveauté en musique," it praised his two most recent works as examples of "un art *nouveau* et *véritable*" ("an art that is *new* and *true*")—two concepts that played an important part in Apollinaire's own aesthetics. The article itself was followed by three scenes from *Les Chants de la mi-mort*, whose music Savinio had played at his concert in May.

Francis Picabia

The relations between Apollinaire and Francis Picabia (fig. 6) are relatively well known. Suffice it to say that they were close

6. Francis Picabia, about 1917. Collection Arensberg Archives, The Francis Bacon Library, Claremont, California.

friends who enjoyed discussing art and literature whenever they were together. The more significant events in their friendship included a trip to England in August 1912, a vacation (with Marcel Duchamp) at the Picabias' property in Etival in October 1912, where Apollinaire recited "Zone" for the first time, and the discovery of Raymond Roussel's *Impressions d'Afrique,* which they attended (also with Duchamp) in either 1911 or 1912. Picabia visited America for the first time in January 1913 in connection with the Armory Show. This revolutionary exhibition included four of his own works, which caused quite a stir. Indeed together with Duchamp, whose paintings were equally scandalous, he quickly became the star of the show. During his stay in New York Picabia struck up a friendship with several important members of the avant-garde, among whom were Alfred Stieglitz, Walter Conrad Arensberg, and Marius de Zayas. Between January and April he visited his friends at "291" practically every day.[13]

Interestingly Picabia also spent considerable time and energy publicizing Apollinaire's *Les Peintres cubistes,* which was published on 17 March while he was still in New York. In particular he persuaded the most important bookstore in town—Brentano's—to order several copies from the publisher.[14] Whenever and wherever he could Picabia publicized Apollinaire and the Orphic painters. It was undoubtedly due to his efforts, for example, that John Weichsel quoted three passages from *Les Peintres cubistes* in the April issue of *Camera Work.*[15] Similarly, in a special issue published in June, Maurice Aisen declared: "The painting of today is but just born; but we are already conscious that it is the emotion of the *réalité* of conception that the new movement tries to produce and not the *réalité* of vision, the painting of yesterday."[16] This distinction was drawn practically verbatim from Apollinaire's book, where it opens the section devoted to the four types of Cubism.

One finds a discussion of these tendencies—scientific, physical, instinctive, and Orphic—a few pages later in the same issue of *Camera Work.* Entitled "Vers l'amorphisme" ("Toward Amorphism"), an anonymous article was reprinted from *Les Hommes du Jour.* Appearing in the original French, the essay introduced Apollinaire's four tendencies and then discussed each category in detail. Elsewhere the author cited the famous phrase: "Un Picasso étudie un objet comme un chirurgien dissèque un cadavre" ("A Picasso analyzes an object as a surgeon dissects a cadaver")—taken as well from *Les Peintres cubistes.* According to William Agee the author of this study was actually Picabia.[17] Before returning to

France the latter exhibited some watercolors at the "291" gallery from 17 March to 5 April 1913. On 10 April he left New York for Paris, imbued with the spirit of Stieglitz's enterprise and determined to open a gallery in Paris based on "291." This project, in which the patron of the arts Mabel Dodge was also involved, was accomplished toward the end of the year. Baptized "L'Ourse" ("The Bear") by its owners, the gallery soon closed its doors for unknown reasons.

In 1914 there were numerous references to the painter in Apollinaire's various newspaper columns. In *L'Intransigeant* on 2 March, for example, he praised "le raffinement un peu sec, mais si précis, si élégant" ("the slightly dry refinement, but so precise, so elegant") of the paintings Picabia had sent to the Salon des Indépendants, adding that "l'influence qu'a déjà exercée ce peintre si combattu nous garantit son importance" ("the influence already exerted by this artistic combat veteran guarantees his importance").[18] The same month he reproduced six of his works in *Les Soirées de Paris*, including two paintings in color. Elsewhere in the same journal he remarked that Picabia's art "grandit, [en devenant] plus concret, plus précis, plus fort et plus délicat que l'an dernier" ("is developing, [becoming] more concrete, more precise, more forceful, and more delicate than last year")[19] In general Apollinaire's references to Picabia followed his aesthetic evolution closely. The poet always seems to have been informed about the painter's latest developments, and his commentary was often situated between the termination of one canvas and the beginning of another. In 1914 this was especially evident in the art column he wrote for *Paris-Journal*. On 29 May, for instance, he mentioned that the artist had sent several recent watercolors to a show in Holland.[20] On 13 July he informed his readers that Picabia had finished two canvases for the Salon d'Automne and that he was preparing a third one.[21] For the present purposes the most interesting column is that dated 25 July 1914:

> En même temps que son *Mariage comique*, Francis Picabia vient d'achever pour le Salon d'Automne une toile extrêmement impressionnante intitulée: *C'est de moi qu'il s'agit*. Ceux qui l'ont vue s'accordent à trouver que c'est là son oeuvre la plus importante. . . .
> Aussitôt sa toile achevée, Picabia est aussitôt parti pour le Jura afin d'y préparer dans la paix des montagnes en collaboration avec Marius de Zayas, des décors pour une pièce qui doit être jouée en Amérique pendant la saison prochaine.
> Ces décors seront certainement quelque chose de nouveau.

(At the same time as his *Comic Marriage*, Francis Picabia has just finished an extremely impressive painting for the Salon d'Automne entitled: *I am the Subject of This Painting*. Those who have seen it agree that it is his most important work. . . .

As soon as his canvas was finished Picabia left for the Jura region to prepare in this peaceful setting, together, with Marius de Zayas, the sets for a play that will be performed in America during the coming season.

These sets will be something entirely new.).[22]

Thus the collaborators were envisioning one or more performances of the pantomime in America! The very idea is stupefying. It is not difficult to imagine the enormous importance that *A quelle heure* would have had for the evolution of the arts in the United States. The project is confirmed, moreover, by a note in the manuscript itself (scene 1) concerning three verses taken from "Le Musicien de Saint-Merry." "Peut-être traduire ces vers en anglais," Apollinaire queried, "ou bien les laisser en français?" ("Perhaps translate these lines into English or leave them in French?"). Further confirmation is provided by another recently discovered text. In his *Souvenirs de la Grande Guerre (Memories of the Great War)*, apparently written toward the end of 1914, Apollinaire described the period immediately preceding the declaration of war:

Entretemps je préparai une pantomime dont j'ai oublié le titre mais dont le sujet était tiré de mon poème "Le Musicien de Saint-Merry," la musique devait être écrite par Albert Savinio, frère du peintre Giorgio de Chirico. Les décors allaient être peints par Picabia et le caricaturiste Marius de Zayas. En attendant le 25 [juillet] je fus sur le point d'aller avec Picabia et Zayas à Etival où ils allaient chez Picabia pour préparer les décors. Car la pantomime devait être jouée au mois de janvier à New York et j'y aurais été aussi. On se promettait grand succès. Les frais devaient être faits par Stieglitz qui serait facilement rentré dans ses fonds à cause de la curiosité que nos noms auraient excitée à Manhattan sur les bords de l'Hudson.

(Meanwhile I prepared a pantomime whose title I have forgotten but whose subject was taken from my poem "Le Musicien de Saint-Merry." The music was to be composed by Albert Savinio, the brother of the painter Giorgio de Chirico. The scenery was going to be painted by Picabia and the caricaturist Marius de Zayas. While I was waiting for [July] 25th I nearly accompanied Picabia and Zayas to Etival where they were going to prepare the scenery at Picabia's place. For the pantomime was to be performed in New York in January, and I would have been there too. We envisioned a great success. The expenses were to be paid by Stieglitz who would easily have advanced the necessary sum due to the curiosity that our names would have aroused in Manhattan on the Hudson).[23]

Thus the performances were to take place under the auspices of Alfred Stieglitz in New York. Conceived from the beginning as a "291" event, *A quelle heure* had been commissioned by Marius de Zayas, who wanted to introduce America to the new aesthetics he had discovered in Paris.[24] From this it is clear that the pantomime was associated with his other projects: the Rousseau exhibition, the book by Apollinaire about the Douanier, the manuscripts of the calligrams, and the African sculptures, all of which were destined for "291" for the same reason. Let us examine the pantomime itself now in an effort to extract the essence of that new aesthetics.

What Times Does A Train Leave For Paris?

Characters
The Musician with no eyes, no nose, and no ears
As many women as possible
The Eiffel Tower
The Arc de Triomphe
Notre Dame
A Tall Factory Chimney
The Sovereign
Two Attendants
The Soldier
The Poet

Scene 1

A screen of white cloth—placed quite near the footlights—fills the whole stage. *The Poet* stands between the screen and the footlights, to one side. We see, crossing the luminous screen, the black silhouettes of the "beings whom the poet does not know but whom he has the right at last to greet." And in effect, the poet greets each passerby with a brief, jerky, automatic gesture.

Then a black curtain falls in front of the screen, hiding even the poet. In complete darkness a powerful voice cries through a megaphone:

"I sing not of this world nor of other stars
I sing the possibilities of myself beyond this world and the stars
I sing the joy of wandering and the pleasure of a wanderer's death."

Scene 2

Against the black curtain, which is still lowered, a strip of white cloth passes horizontally (from right to left) on which is written the following date: the 21st day of the month on May 1913 (the letters are all capitals, black, and printed on a press rather than by hand; the numbers are red).

In the distance we hear the faceless musician's flute.

The black curtain is raised. We see millions of flies flying about a luminous column (this set is a little closer to the rear of the stage than the screen in scene 1, but not too far from the footlights).

Then the lights go down for a moment.

When the lights come back up, we see the city very low in the background, almost at stage level: rooftops; smoking chimneys, both tall and short (this set will be placed at the back of the stage). Trees serve to fill out the background. The *Eiffel Tower,* the *Arc de Triomphe, Notre Dame, A Tall Factory Chimney.* Near the right wing the silhouette of a black hand is printed on the wall. This hand points to a nearby placard, which reads: "rue Aubry-le-Boucher."

The man with no eyes, no nose, and no ears enters from the left. He crosses the stage slowly, then enters the street indicated by the placard and disappears (according to lines 11 and 12 of the poem).

The Eiffel Tower projects images into the audience. The sounds of city life: automobile horns, bells, klaxons, the crackling of wireless telegraphy, shouts represented by:

"When I was a child there were no automobiles."
VOICES: "Help!"—"An airplane is buzzing us."
"Long live liberty!"—"We are leaving for America."

Scene 3

A small square. A fountain on the left. In the background, the *Eiffel Tower, Notre Dame,* the *Arc de Triomphe,* and the *Tall Factory*

Chimney. Several streets, indicated by placards, intersect the small square: "rue Aubry-le-Boucher," "rue Saint-Martin," "rue Simon-le-Franc."

The Man with no eyes, no nose, and no ears advances slowly, entering on the right and playing his flute. He has no mouth but plays the flute through an opening in his throat covered by a rubber or metal washer, like those applied to horses following surgery on their respiratory tracts. He soon comes to a halt (near the right wing). While he continues to play, various *women* gradually gather around him: a woman with no head, a woman with no arms, a blue woman, a red woman, a bald woman, a smartly dressed woman, a little girl, an old woman. Several attractive whores, some women with long hair, some nude women (wearing tights).

When they have all assembled the Man walks slowly to the fountain, followed by the women. The church bell rings. The Man ceases playing his flute and drinks from the fountain. The women crowd around in order to look at him, in order to seize him.

Then the Man resumes his melody and retraces his steps, followed by the women. More women arrive from several different directions, with a wild look in their eyes, their hands stretched out before them. The music fades away in the distance.

Scene 4

While the flute music is fading away a curtain falls in the background and hides the monuments. Either a light show or moving pictures illustrates the theme of life and its variety: Trains leaving the station—Tropical birds and vegetation—Equatorial Africa's Panic religious life—Smoothly flowing European rivers—Life in the small, fresh towns of central France—The European night traversed by freight trains—European urban life—And some scenes with tall chimneys.

Then, accompanied by music and projections, the history of Paris with its ancient processions. A troop of hatters, banana pedlars, and *especially* some Republican Guardsmen. The king passes wearing a modern costume: Napoleon III with two attendants.

Scene 5

A Paris street. Between center stage and the right wing is an ancient house with broken windows for sale. Its front door is open. *The Musician* arrives from the left and enters the house, followed by the women. Before entering they cry out their names: Ariadne, Pâquerette, Anne, Mia, Simone, Mavise, Colette, Geneviève, Louise, Julie, and Armande.

Two men—*a soldier* and *a poet*—arrive from opposite directions. They hear the music and the sounds made by the women. Surprised and apparently frightened, they halt in their tracks and wait.

The music fades away. Night falls. The soldier and the poet, who remain behind, seem to be searching for something. The door of the house is locked. They break in the door and open it. [The musician and the women have vanished. The house is deserted.]

Scene 6

Then the scene changes, and we are back at the small square of scene 3. *The Man* has returned to his place on the right. *The soldier* and *the poet* enter by a door on the left and catch sight of him. *The automatic sovereign* crosses the stage with *his attendants*, who are blowing their noses.

The sovereign commits suicide with one shot from his revolver.
The End

From the Poem to the Pantomime

It should be noted at the outset that another text by Apollinaire forms a sort of bridge between "Le Musicien de Saint-Merry" and *A quelle heure un train partira-t-il pour Paris?* Entitled "Un dernier chapitre" ("A Last Chapter"), it was given to Ardengo Soffici early in 1914, while he was in Paris, and appeared in *Lacerba* on 1 June of that year:

Tout le peuple se précipita sur la place publique
Il vint des hommes blancs des nègres des jaunes et quelques rouges
Il vint des ouvriers des usines dont les hautes cheminées
    ne fumaient plus à cause de la grève

Il vint des maçons aux vêtements maculés de plâtre
Il vint des garçons bouchers aux bras teints de sang
Des mitrons pales de la farine qui les saupoudrait
Et des commis de commerçants de toutes sortes
Il vint des femmes terribles et portant des enfants ou en ayant d'autres accrochés à leurs jupes
Il vint des femmes pauvres mais effrontées plâtrées maquillées aux gestes étranges
Il vint des estropiés des aveugles des culs-de-jatte des manchots des boiteux
Il vint même des prêtres et quelques hommes mis avec élégance
Et hors la place la ville semblait morte ne tressaillant même pas

(All the people rushed to the public square
There came men who were white black yellow and red
There came some workers from factories whose tall chimneys had stopped smoking because of the strike
There came some masons whose clothes were smeared with plaster
There came some apprentice butchers whose arms were covered with blood
Some apprentice bakers sprinkled with flour
And clerks from all sort of businesses
There came some terrible women carrying children or with others clinging to their skirts
There came some poor but broken women with strange gestures and plastered with makeup
There came men who were crippled blind legless limping or lacking an arm
There even came some priests and men wearing elegant clothes
And outside the square the town seemed dead and not even quivering.)[25]

Among the various features that recall the earlier poem one notes the anaphora "Il vint," the milling throng, and the brazen women who resemble the prostitutes in "Le Musicien de Saint-Merry." Whereas the women in that poem hold their arms stretched out before them, those in "Un dernier chapitre" make "gestes étranges." In both cases they have a wild look in their eyes. Similarly, the priests and the elegantly dressed men recall the priest from the Eglise de Saint-Merry and the ambassadors who used to pass through the quarter whenever they arrived in Paris. The strike and the baker's apprentices covered with flour evoke the bakers in the Saint-Merry quarter, as well, who were also on strike. Finally, the two poems end with the image of an abandoned city, haunted by death. It is interesting to note that the experience described in "Un dernier chapitre" is identical to the description provided by Jean Mollet, who evoked a walk that he and Apollinaire took in the same part of town. "Les rues étaient complètement vides," he recalled, "pas un chat, pas une voiture . . . nous aperçumes dans une cour un musicien et un chanteur entourés d'une foule de gens qui répétaient en choeur le refrain d'une chanson. On aurait cru que toutes les rues s'étaient vidées dans cette cour" ("The streets were completely empty, nary a cat, nary a car . . . in a courtyard we perceived a musician and a singer surrounded by a bunch of people who were all repeating the refrain of a song. You would have thought that all the streets emptied into that courtyard").[26] With regard to the pantomime one naturally thinks of the white, black, yellow, and red men, who prefigure the women painted different colors. In addition it is worth noting the "usines dont les hautes cheminées ne fumaient plus," which anticipate the Tall Factory Chimney and various other chimneys in the pantomime.

To be sure, one also observes several differences between "Le Musicien de Saint-Merry" and *A quelle heure*. Whereas in the poem the witnesses of the infernal drama are Apollinaire (the narrator) and a priest, in the pantomime the witnesses are a poet and a soldier. Apollinaire may have decided to discard the priest for any one of several reasons. Perhaps he simply wished to avoid the risks connected with portraying an ecclesiastic on stage, especially in a play that sought to provoke a *succès de scandale*. And for a quarter with a long history of prostitution what better replacement than a soldier—a member of the Republican Guard at that? However, the greatest difference derives from the important role played by surprise in *A quelle heure,* in contrast to the mystery that predominantes in the poem. It is enough to compare the two conclusions to grasp this distinction. Although the pantomime follows the poem's plot fairly closely, even displaying the date and the names of the streets mentioned in "Le Musicien de Saint-Merry," the two works are entirely distinct from one another. Their difference also stems from the use of projections and from special lighting effects, even though all this is authorized by the poem. The pantomime's simultanism, its evocation of life's infinite variety ("And while the world was living and fluctuating"), the history of the Saint-Merry quarter—all this was present in the poem and is simply dramatized on the stage

In general *A quelle heure* is a faithful adaptation of the original poem. In adapting it for the stage Apollinaire succeeded in translating the original poetic language into the type of vocabulary demanded by the theater. If the pantomime follows its model closely, it adds numerous details that make it more immediate and more concrete. These include the airplane ("An airplane is buzzing us") and the Tall Factory Chimney. In particular these objects confirm Philippe Renaud's suspicion that the lines in the poem: "Those tall chimneys shaped like towers / We are going higher now and no longer touch the ground" (vv. 52–53) evoke factory smokestacks and an airplane ride. The pantomime also confirms March Poupon's thesis that the following verse is a metaphoric description of the moon and the stars: "Millions of flies were fanning a splendor." For if these flies actually exist in the theatrical version, the expression "tandis que le jour renaît" ("while morning dawns")—which Apollinaire added to the second scene but eventually crossed out—indicates that the story begins just before dawn. Moreover, a ballet version composed at a later date begins with a musical prelude on the themes of Night, the Stars, and the Immensity of Existence. To be sure, the flies' metaphoric value does not rule out additional interpretation at other levels. The same thing can be said of the "splendor" fanned by the flies at the beginning. If the latter image represents the moon on the one hand, it is related to the fable of "The Pied Piper of Hamlin" on the other. Present here in the form of a luminous column, it recalls the column that bore the names of the children enticed away by the infernal musician.

The Faceless Man

The sources of Apollinaire's hero have already been discussed as well as his multiple meanings. As noted, the musician's physical appearance is governed by two contradictory constants: the absence of any physiognomy and the presence of a mouth—displaced here to the region of the throat. One is left with a human body crowned by a smooth, spherical head—whence its phallic symbolism. Reviewing *Le Poète assassiné* in 1916, Alberto Savinio provided some additional information about this character's costume. Neglecting the subject he was supposedly discussing, Savinio devoted the entire first page not to the novel but to the collaboration on the pantomime:

> Canicole del '14. . . . In quattro, nel paccobotto edilizio di Guillaume Apollinaire. . . . tratteggiavamo le scene di una teatralità che avrebe intonacato cinque fra le più cospicue città degli U.S.A.: A

quelle heure un train partira-t-il pour Paris?—titolo lunghetto per le tradizioni del cartellone a successo . . . ma poema di Apollinaire, scenari di Picabia, musica di Savinio, messinscena di Zayas. . . .

Non ci s'accomunava nemmeno sulla figura del protagonista: farlo apparire con il viso imbottito di stoppa, con la cucitura che gli scendesse guì dall'occipite sino alla ganascia come una grossa vena? . . . oppure sintetizzarlo in un grappolo di lampadine volitanti?

(The dog-days of 1914. . . Four of us gathered together in the ship-like apartment of Guillaume Apollinaire. . . . We were sketching the scenes of a theatrical event that would have amazed five of the most important cities in the U.S.A.: *A quelle heure un train partira-t-il pour Paris*—the lengthy title coming from the traditional use of placards in a series . . . poem by Apollinaire, scenery by Picabia, music by Savinio, staging by de Zayas. . . .

We couldn't even agree on the protagonist's appearance: should he appear on stage with his face stuffed with oakum and a seam running from his occiput to his jawline like a large vein? . . . or should he be represented by a fluttering cluster of lightbulbs?.[27]

The manner in which the poem was staged, the costume described by Savinio—these would have underlined the hero's sex-

7. Fantômas, from Louis Feuillade's film *Fantômas,* 1913.

ual aspect. For there is no doubt that the cluster of lightbulbs would have been abandoned in favor of the other, much more explicit costume. Swollen with blood, the large vein would have suggested, first, a vein in the forehead standing out during sexual intercourse and, secondly, the male member in a state of erection.

Although the details are sketchy, Apollinaire's phallomorphic protagonist seems to be related to the archcriminal Fantômas, the hero of numerous films by Louis Feuillade during this period. In *Fantômas* (fig. 7), for example, he wore a black hood that effectively hid his features. Significantly this film dates from 1913, the year of the supposed encounter between the musician and the "Merry widows." Fantômas wore a similar costume in *L'Homme sans visage (The Faceless Man)* (1919), whose title recalls the "faceless musician" in *A quelle heure*.[28] As is well known, the poet was a great admirer of this character, whose name graced the pages of *Les Soirées de Paris* on several occasions. In 1914, discussing the book *Fantômas* (the source of the films) in the *Mercure de France*, Apollinaire noted that the novel was extremely popular in certain literary and artistic circles. He even went so far as to say: "*Fantômas* est, au point de vue imaginatif, une des oeuvres les plus riches qui existent" ("As far as imagination is concerned *Fantômas* is one of the richest works in existence").[29] Less well known is Apollinaire's fascination with the *cagoule*, a cloth hood with holes for the mouth and eyes. In a letter to Madeleine Pagès on 15 September 1915, for example, he described the following incident from his childhood:

> La cagoule est une chose qui a vivement frappé mon enfance. Je suis . . . né à Rome et je suis venu en France à l'âge de 3 ans. Mais je me souviens fort bien d'une certaine confrérie qu'on voyait aux enterrements et dont les membres avaient tous des cagoules. Cela m'épouvantait un peu.

> (The *cagoule* had a vivid impact on my childhood. I was . . . born in Rome and came to France when I was 3. But I remember a certain religious brotherhood very well whose members were often seen at funerals and who wore hoods. That frightened me a little.[30]

Without being able to prove it, one suspects that Fantômas was yet another source for the musician of Saint-Merry. However, while the two characters resemble each other in several respects, nothing in the series of novels devoted to the archcriminal recurs in Apollinaire's poem (or pantomime). Likewise, one notes an important distinction between Fantômas and the musician. In the first instance one is confronted with a man who wears a disguise, who simply wishes to conceal his face. In the second instance one finds oneself in the presence of a man who really *has no face*.

Symbol, Rite, and Magic

In support of the previous sexual interpretation it should be added that the pantomime contains numerous sexual symbols, most of which are elevated to monumental status. If "Le Musicien de Saint-Merry" includes numerous examples, one finds even more of them in *A quelle heure*. Among the masculine symbols should be grouped the magic flute, the industrial smokestacks, the bananas, and the musician himself—supplemented in the pantomime by the luminous column, the Tall Factory Chimney, and, naturally, the Eiffel Tower.[31] As before, the feminine symbols include the fountain, the various women, the open door, the broken windows, and the empty house that engulfs the procession at the end. In the pantomime, however, their number is increased by two feminine monuments: the Arc de Triomphe and Notre Dame cathedral. Judging from the conspicuousness and quantity of these symbols, Apollinaire must have attached considerable importance to them. This is especially true of the four ambulatory monuments, whose presence is felt throughout the pantomime. Omnipresent guardians of the basic principles of life, they reflect a belief in a dualistic universe governed by sexual forces. In this context one thinks of a remark by Jean Levaillant who, referring to the calligrams in general, declared: "Ainsi l'espace recèle une tension, un appel des formes vers les formes, une dynamique incessante du désir" ("Thus the space conceals a tension, an attraction of forms to other forms, an incessant dynamics of desire").[32] By translating this dynamics into theatrical terms *A quelle heure* illustrates his thesis perfectly.

Two observations suggest themselves concerning the sexualized universe in the pantomime. First of all, it seems doubtful that Apollinaire ever bothered to explain the work to his three collaborators. On the contrary, he appears to have wanted to preserve its air of mystery, especially with regard to his hero's phallic identity. Second, in the absence of a detailed explanation the collaborators were forced to interrogate the text itself, from which they derived an interpretation that dovetailed with the author's intentions. Among other things, they observed the sexual symbolism and realized that the pantomime depicted the drama of sexuality. This impression is reinforced by a document belonging to the Marius de Zayas Archives in Seville. It is a partial manuscript of *A quelle heure* comprising some four pages. Following the title page and the list of characters, one encounters two sheets reproducing scenes 5 and 6 (labeled "Scéne IV" and "Scéne V"). Copied in de Zayas's handwriting, this version is slightly earlier than the manuscript in the Francis Bacon Library. Toward the beginning of scene 6 de Zayas appended a long note concerning the faceless man.

> Je pense souvent à ce malheureux que l'amour a banni de son royaume et qui, poussé par les commandements de la nature, cherche éternellement la consolation de ses maux dans la satisfaction de ses désirs barrés. Et je bénis le bordel car c'est le baume des blessures de ce grand crucifié qui s'appelle l'homme. Je pense souvent aux femmes indigentes qui sont enceintes, qui n'auront pas de lit pour accoucher de l'être qui leur déchire le ventre. Et je bénis les maisons de maternité car elles sont le baume des blessures de cette grande douloureuse qui s'appelle la femme. Et je pense aussi qu'il y a des cerveaux qui sont bannis de la joie de vivre parce qu'ils ne sont pas compris. Car la compréhension c'est la cohabitation de deux cerveaux.
>
> (I often think of that sad individual whom love has banished from his kingdom and who, responding to nature's commands, eternally seeks consolation for his misfortune in the satisfaction of his thwarted desires. And I bless the brothel, for it is balm to the wounds of that great crucified being known as man. I often think of poor women who are pregnant, who will have no bed in which to give birth to the creature who is tearing at their belly. And I bless the maternity hospitals, for they are balm to the wounds of that long suffering being known as woman. And I also think there are some minds that are banished from life's joy because they are not understood. For understanding is the cohabitation of two minds.)

This passage demonstrates that de Zayas conceived of the faceless man as a sympathetic character. For him the faceless man symbolized the masculine condition, driven by a sexual desire that he succeeded only rarely in satisfying. It is evident as well that this interpretation approximated Apollinaire's own response. In both cases it was a question of a phallic individual who was obsessed with the sexual act. But de Zayas's meditation went far beyond the subject of the faceless man. To the latter he juxtaposed the image of the feminine condition, woman writhing in pain during childbirth. Like man, she was crucified by the sexual forces that governed her life. In the last analysis it was the drama of sexuality and the drama of fertility that interested de Zayas. Once again this interpretation did not differ appreciably from Apollinaire's own understanding.

The full value of Apollinaire's sexual symbols would appear to stem from their connection with certain fertility rites, with ceremonies intended to assure the fecundity of the earth or of a group of women. As has been seen previously, these rites often involve some form of phallic worship. In this instance the women who follow the musician of Saint-Merry in a hypnotic state represent worshippers fallen in ecstasy before the sacred phallus. Among other things fertility rites are commonly performed during the spring, which may explain why the action takes place in May. Not only does Apollinaire evoke the Greek ceremony, the phallic procession in honor of Dionysos, but he alludes to African rites as well. For one thing, in "Le Musicien de Saint-Merry" line 37 comments on religious sculpture in the Belgian Congo: "Catholic mission in Boma what have you done with the sculptor?" For another, this impression is reinforced by a reference to African ceremonies in *A quelle heure*. Among the subjects chosen to represent life's infinite variety, evoked by projections and other special effects, Apollinaire specifically cites "Equatorial Africa's Panic religious life." The curious adjective *panique* serves to link the Negro rites to Greek legends concerning death and rebirth. And yet the epithet seems poorly suited to describe life in Africa until one realizes that it has nothing to do with fear. On the contrary, Apollinaire has restored its etymological meaning, which is associated with the god Pan. The term serves to designate a lifestyle resembling Pan's, one that is voluptuous, pastoral, and musical.

This reference recalls suggestions by various critics that the Musician of Saint-Merry should be viewed as an avatar of Pan as well. More important, however, is the fact that Apollinaire connects Pan with African religion, that is, with statuettes employed in the African ceremonies. The association of ideas, characters, and objects that apparently have nothing in common is actually one of the constants in Apollinaire's work. The Pan/statuettes configuration, whose sources sprang from the depths of his unconscious, existed at least as early as 1909, the date of the following description of some fetishes belonging to Matisse:

> Il aime à s'entourer . . . de ces sculptures où les nègres de la Guinée, du Sénégal et du Gabon ont figuré avec une rare pureté leurs passions les plus paniques.

(He loves to surround himself . . . with those sculptures in which the Negroes of Guinea, Sénégal, and Gabon have expressed, with rare purity, their most Panic passions.)[33]

Apollinaire himself was extremely interested in African and Polynesian sculpture. In the course of his readings he must certainly have come across descriptions of fertility rites performed in those regions. In turn he may well have been inspired by one of these ceremonies to create "Le Musicien de Saint-Merry." Or again it may have been the sculpture itself that provided the inspiration. His protagonist, and even much of the plot, could easily have stemmed from the observation that the male idols usually were endowed with prominent members. It is possible therefore that the faceless man was inspired, at least partially, by a sculpture in a Parisian collection. Perhaps an object such as the smooth, faceless statuette from the Caroline Islands that is pictured in André Breton's *L'art magique*.[34] Although the extent of Apollinaire's debt to African art is difficult to determine, he was obviously struck by the statues' sexuality.[35] Discussing Archipenko's sculpture, for example, he demonstrated an excellent knowledge of African art. In this context he evoked "la multitude des dieux enfin qui [reflètent] symboliquement les phénomènes de la nature" ("the multitude of gods who [reflect] natural phenomena symbolically"), while underlining the role of the "dieux de la guerre et du semen avec des organes génitaux énormes" ("gods of war and of semen with enormous genitals")[36] In addition, in his poem "Les Grands Fétiches" (1916) Blaise Cendrars described an African sculpture that resembled Apollinaire's protagonist: "Lui / Chauve / N'a qu'une bouche / Un membre qui descend aux genoux." ("Bald / He / Has only a mouth / An organ that hangs down to his knees.")[37]

Although the so-called "primitive" religions employ a considerable amount of sexual symbolism, it is generally in a passive manner, for example in their mythology. In fertility rites, however, this symbolism becomes active and capable of influencing material events. In a sense the distinction between symbol and object symbolized vanishes as soon as one assumes that the interaction of symbols—manipulated artificially—will produce a parallel interaction of the corresponding objects in nature. This is the basic assumption of all imitative magic, an assumption that also underlies the sexual symbolism in the pantomime. While Apollinaire doubtless did not believe in the magical efficacy of his symbols, it is important to note that he uses them as if he actually did. In effect ritual assumed a generative function in the origin of *A quelle heure* to such an extent that the distinction between the two modes of expression—magical and symbolic—tends to disappear. The erotic mixing of male and female symbols is perhaps more comprehensible if one translates the principle of imitative magic into psychological terms: it is clearly an example of wish fulfillment. For, as John Beattie observes, speaking of anthropology, "magic is the acting out of a situation, the expression of a desire in symbolic terms."[38] Thus the story of the musician of Saint-Merry is as much as anything a product of the poet's own libido. On one level at least it represents a dramatization of the sexual tensions, of the psychological preoccupations of Apollinaire. He frankly admits, at the beginning of both the poem and the pantomime, that what one is about to see is his internal life, where fantasy is king: "I sing the possibilities of myself beyond this world and the stars."[39] One is thus confronted with a grandiose sexual fantasy on the part of Apollinaire in which a personification of his own sexual member plays the starring role, an example of phallic narcissism translated into artistic terms. It should be added that Beattie's definition applies to myth as well as to magic, which explains why the pantomime's mythic dimension is closely linked to its magic and symbolic aspects.

From Futurism to Dada

In contrast to its multivalent signification, the plot of *A quelle heure* is relatively simple. For the most part it is modeled on that of the poem. The single exception is the final scene, created specifically for the pantomime, which introduces an unexpected character. Napoleon III (here called an "automatic sovereign") crosses the stage with two attendants who are blowing their noses. Without any preparation, or visible provocation, he commits suicide with a single shot from his revolver. This conclusion, a sort of dramatic non sequitur, is as enigmatic as it is shocking. Apollinaire seems to have had but one purpose, namely to scandalize the audience and provoke a general (probably violent) expression of outrage. This of course was a time-honored goal of avant-garde drama since Alfred Jarry's *Ubu roi*. In 1916, moreover, it was to become one of the tenets of the Dada movement.

And yet, despite the conclusion's obvious absurdity, it is more coherent than one would have believed. According to the perspective one adopts, it lends itself to several interpretations. It is probable, for example, that this scene summarizes a whole philosophy. For if the automatic sovereign's suicide is absurd, this is because death itself is absurd. The eventual goal of all life, it is entirely gratuitous—like existence itself. In the last analysis, therefore, the ending underlines the paradox of the human condition. On another level a certain symmetry emerges between the conclusion and the pantomime's opening scene, where one encounters millions of flies flying around a luminous column. One thinks in particular of the two attendants who accompany the sovereign, for their behavior is extremely curious. Nevertheless, as Peter Read has observed, it is no accident that the attendants are blowing their noses ("se mouchent"). A sort of visual pun, this action repeats the theme of the infernal insects ("mouches") evoked at the beginning. Thus the pantomime opens and closes with the image of Beelzebub, Lord of the Flies, who is identified first with the faceless musician, then with the automatic sovereign. The latter character's suicide would be explained on this level by his desire to return to his infernal kingdom. Killing himself is simply the easiest way to return to Hell—through the agency of his own death.

At yet another level the automatic sovereign represents a historical figure: Napoleon III. Together with his attendants, this character has already been encountered during the simultanist episode in the fourth scene. The personal associations that Napoleon III had for Apollinaire are difficult to determine, but one suspects that this figure's suicide requires a historical or a political interpretation. Among other things it recalls a line from "Vendémiaire": "Je vivais à l'époque où finissaient les rois" ("I lived at the time when the kings were dying out"), which suggests another poem as well. "Coeur couronne et miroir" contains the following verse: "Les rois qui meurent tour à tour renaissent au coeur des poètes" ("The kings who are dying one by one are reborn in the hearts of the poets"). Napoleon III was of course the last of the French rulers. Accordingly, it seems that the death of the king, which parallels the death (disappearance) of the women, constitutes a coherent ending after all. It appears to be part of a parallel structure extending throughout the entire play. Just as the disappearance of the musician and his women terminates the spatial procession structuring the pantomime, the suicide terminates the temporal procession led by the king and his followers that extends across the centuries. At the end this royal personage passes in effect from the past to the present where, as

Apollinaire noted, the institution of monarchy was fast disappearing. It is precisely his entry into the twentieth century, therefore, that is responsible for his death, that makes his death inevitable. At the very end of the pantomime the faceless musician is the only character left, having abandoned his female followers in Hell/Hades and returned to earth. It is he, in his role as a modern Orpheus, who finally replaces the automatic sovereign. The latter, according to Apollinaire's dictum, is thus "reborn" in the heart of a poet.

To be sure, Apollinaire was not the first to make use of automatic characters in the theater. Among the various antecedants Jarry's *Ubu roi* should be mentioned, as well as *Les Chants de la mimort* by Alberto Savinio—two works whose influence is felt throughout the pantomime. Except for the last scene the most important innovations concern the costumes and the stage directions. Apollinaire would seem to have been influenced in particular by the Italian Futurists, most of whom he knew personally. One finds, for example, in his *L'Anti-tradition futuriste* (29 June 1913) the seeds of numerous ideas in the pantomime, ranging from "Danse travail ou chorégraphie pure" to "Mimique universelle et Art des lumières" ("Dance labor or pure choreography, Universal Mimicry, and the Art of lights").[40] While this manifesto was conceived as a summary of the avant-garde tendencies of the day, it also included the proclamations issued by the Futurists up to that point. Thus Apollinaire's advocacy of a "vie captivée ou phonocinématographie" ("captivated life or phonocinematography") was mostly his own idea, but the recommendation of a "musique totale et *Art des bruits*" (Total music and *Art of noises*") was taken directly from Luigi Russolo's manifesto *L'Arte dei Rumori (The Art of Noises)* (11 March 1913), in which the latter foresaw a new kind of music based on six different types of noise. It is worth noting that both these ideas are realized to some extent in *A quelle heure,* where certain noises are synchronized with certain projections. Thus the moving pictures projected by the Eiffel Tower in scene 2 are accompanied by "the sounds of city life: automobile horns, bells, klaxons, the crackling of wireless telegraphy." This aesthetic would find its ultimate expression in *Les Mamelles de Tirésias* in 1917.

In this respect the following paragraph presents considerable interest. It is taken from one of F. T. Marinetti's manifestos, written three months after Apollinaire's and entitled *Il Teatro di Varietà (The Variety Theater).*

Il Teatro di Varietà è il solo che utilizzi oggi il cinematografo, che lo arricchisa d'un numero incalcolabile di visioni e di spettacoli irrealizzabili (battaglie, tumulti, corse, circuiti d'automobili e d'aeroplani, viaggi, transatlantici, profondità di città, di campagne, d'oceani e di cieli).

(The Variety Theater is the only theater today using cinematography, which enriches it with innumerable visions and spectacles that are unrealizable on the stage (battles, riots, races, automobile and airplane races, voyages, oceanliners, the depths of cities, of the countryside, of the oceans, and of the heavens.)

This pronouncement must have greatly interested Apollinaire, who read Marinetti's manifesto as soon as it appeared. Writing in the section of *Les Soirèes de Paris* entitled "Chronique mensuelle" on 15 November 1913, he remarked:

Tandis que Marinetti souhaite l'ouverture d'un Théâtre de Variété où les acteurs ne seraient qu'acrobates, clowns et danseurs, tandis que les spectateurs s'y démèneraient, y crieraient, jouant chacun un rôle improvisé, à l'instar de la Commedia dell Arte, M. Jacques Copeau vient d'ouvrir le Théâtre du Vieux-Colombier.

(While Marinetti yearns for a Variety Theater in which the actors would consist of acrobats, clowns, and dancers, while the spectators would carry on, would utter loud cries, each one playing an improvised role, modeled on the Commedia dell'Arte, M. Jacques Copeau has just founded the Théâtre du Vieux-Colombier.)

It is worth recalling that Apollinaire had noted one year previously that the cinema could easily outdo the theater when it came to realistic stage effects.[4] Here in effect was a solution to the dilemma in which the modern theater found itself: to incorporate the more realistic and practically limitless "resources scéniques" of film into the narrower, essentially antirealistic framework of the theater. The possibilities of this new form were endless, as Apollinaire seems to have realized. As Marinetti advocated, he reserved the projections for events that could not readily be represented on the stage. And while eschewing the subjects of war, fighting, and racing so dear to the Futurists, he did in fact use several themes suggested in the manifesto: voyages, machines, city life, and life in the countryside. If he neglected the "oceans" and the "heavens," it was because he preferred to concentrate on history and geography, using the camera to achieve an unparalleled degree of simultaneity—comparable to that of D. W. Griffith's film *Intolerance*, which appeared two years later.

Apollinaire correctly saw that film permitted much more simultaneity than any other medium, especially coupled with a soundtrack. In *A quelle heure* he used the camera as an extension of his body, as a sort of sixth (or seventh) sense that allowed him to overcome the limitations of historical time and geographical space. Or more precisely, to telescope them to a nearly simultaneous point corresponding to the focal point in the brain where consciousness and memory intersect. Apollinaire set himself essentially the same task, therefore, as Griffith in 1916; who attempted a geographical and historical survey of the entire human race. Apollinaire limited his historical survey to Paris, but otherwise his efforts were identical: to capture life in all its diversity and complexity. That he tried to accomplish this in the space of a brief pantomime testifies to his audacity as much as to his ambition.

To Apollinaire's thorough familiarity with Futurism should be added the fact that in the spring of 1914 Paris was invaded by many of the Futurists themselves. A survey of P. A. Jannini's *La fortuna di Apollinaire in Italia* indicates that these included Umberto Boccioni, Carlo Carrà, Aldo Palazzeschi, Ardengo Soffici, Giovanni Papini, and Alberto Magnelli, all of whom visited Apollinaire at one time or another during their stay.[42] Several even found lodging in the offices of *Les Soirées de Paris*. And with Giorgio de Chirico and Alberto Savinio both living in Paris, Apollinaire was subject to a considerable amount of Italian influence at this time. Significantly, he gave birth to two new Italianate genres during this period: the calligram and surrealist drama.

A quelle heure also presents many dadaist aspects that suggest it may reflect Picabia's influence as well. One thinks of the poet who salutes with an automatic (mechanical) gesture, of the absurd conclusion, of the choice of a title having no connection with the story, of the automatic sovereign (Napoleon III) and his noseblowing followers, of the faceless protagonist and the bizarre women who pursue him, and of the rubber washer that the latter wears on his throat. In addition the perverse humor characterizing much of the pantomime resembles the sort of *humour noir* that was to become a Picabia trademark. Nevertheless, while some of these themes are reflected in Picabia's poetry and painting, there is nothing here that can be identified specifically with his work. It should be noted that Picabia's interest in Dada (or pre-Dada) does not seem to have begun before 1915, when it found its first expression in a series of mechanomorphic drawings executed in

New York. On the other hand, these characteristics are manifest in several of Apollinaire's works that are contemporary with the pantomime. The perverse humor, for example, is represented by his "Banalités" and "Quelconqueries," several of which were even collected by André Breton for his *Anthologie de l'humour noir*. The astonishing novel *Le Poète assassiné* (which was finished in 1914) contains a number of examples of *humour noir*—in particular a dadaist playlet entitled *Iéximal Jélimite*, in which, as Marie-Jeanne Durry remarks, "l'humour joue sur un dépaysement, une dissociation des éléments, une rupture du continu" ("the humor depends on a sort of alienation, a dissociation of elements, a rupture of the continuous"),[43] Like *A quelle heure*, moreover, this playlet is sharply delineated, violent, and shocking. Both works exemplify Apollinaire's preoccupation with the antirealistic aesthetic he called "surnaturalisme" in 1914 and later renamed "surréalisme." The dominant characteristic and motivating principle of this aesthetic—which Apollinaire especially associated with drama—were contained in the concept of *surprise*.

It is significant that the bizarre female characters in the pantomime were prefigured by two separate antecedents, neither of which had anything to do with Picabia. It seems, for example, that the concept of dyeing women different hues came originally from the Futurists. Once agian the key text is the long manifesto by Marinetti entitled *Il Teatro di Varietà* (29 September 1913). Buried in the middle of this document is an interesting paragraph concerning dramatic theory and practice:

> Bisogna assolutamente distruggere ogni logica negli spettacoli del Teatro di Varietà, esagerarvi singolarmente il lusso, moltiplicare i contrasti e far regnare sovrani sulla scene l'inverosimile e l'assurdo. (Esempio: Obbligare le chanteuses a tingersi il décolleté, le braccia, e specialmente i capelli, in tutti i colori finora transcurati come mezzi de seduzione. Capelli verdi, braccia violette, décolleté azzurro, chignon arancione, ecc.
>
> (All logical connections must be destroyed in Variety Theater productions while greatly exaggerating their luxury, multiplying their contrasts, and allowing the unlikely and the absurd to reign on stage. (Example: Female singers could be obliged to dye their necks and shoulders, their arms, and especially their hair in every color neglected previously as a means of seduction. Green hair, violet arms, blue neck and shoulders, orange *chignon*, etc.)

Since Apollinaire is known to have read Marinetti's manifesto when it appeared, he was obviously familiar with this passage, which must have greatly amused him. Indeed what one retains more than anything else is the document's outrageous sense of humor. Designed to shock its audience into the twentieth century, the Variety Theater introduced one absurdity after another. There is little doubt in any case that the red and blue woman in *A quelle heure* were inspired by the Futurists. While the women could have been suggested by the passage quoted above, Apollinaire seems in fact to have taken the idea from Alberto Savinio, who borrowed it from Marinetti (see chapter 4). The fact that the musician's followers are red, white (flesh color), and blue may have been an ironic commentary on patriotic womanhood.

Despite his debt to the Variety Theater, Apollinaire was perfectly capable of creating the other bizarre women himself. One has only to glance at the following stanza from "Un Fantôme de nuées" ("A Cloud Phantom"), for example, to see that he was experimenting with similar themes the year before:

> Le second saltimbanque
> N'était vêtu que de son ombre
> Je le regardai longtemps
> Son visage m'échappe entièrement
> C'est un homme sans tête
>
> (The second mountebank
> Was dressed only in his shadow
> I observed him for a long time
> His face escapes me entirely
> He is a man with no head)

It is interesting that this poem was written at the same time as "Le Musicien de Saint-Merry." But one can trace these images back much further, back to "L'Emigrant de Landor Road," which features the same combination of nudity and headlessness:

> Le chapeau à la main il entra du pied droit
> Chez un tailleur très chic et fournisseur du roi
> Ce commerçant venait de couper quelques têtes
> De mannequins vêtus comme il faut qu'on se vête
> . . . .
> Les mannequins pour lui s'étant déshabillées
> Battirent leurs habits puis lui essayèrent.
> (Hat in hand and right foot first he entered
> A fashionable tailor's shop by appointment to the king

> The proprietor had just decapitated several
> Mannequins which were elegantly dressed
> . . . .
> Having undressed on his behalf the mannequins
> Dusted off their clothes and tried them on him.

Despite the various influences that converge on *A quelle heure*, in the last analysis it is very much Apollinaire's own work. A dramatic synthesis of his experience and aesthetic theories, it is stamped with the author's personality throughout and leads directly to the revolutionary play *Les Mamelles de Tirésias* (see chapter 6). The fact that this avant-garde creation dates from (July) 1914 makes it especially interesting. For it is evident that it prefigures—that indeed it predicts—the appearance of the Dada movement a full two years before the term "Dada" was coined.[44] This is actually not terribly surprising since all four collaborators were to become involved in this movement to different degrees, were indeed to help determine the form it would take. Picabia was destined to play a role in its development whose importance would be equaled only by that of Tristan Tzara. It is apparent in any case that Apollinaire's influence on Dada was much greater than anyone has realized. Given the identities of the four collaborators, one feels justified in claiming for *A quelle heure* the role and title of "The First Dada Play." It is an exciting work, both visually and conceptually, exemplifying Apollinaire's preoccupation with newness, modernity, simultaneity, spontaneity, juxtaposition, and—"le ressort le plus modern" ("the newest principle of all")—surprise. There is, moreover, a sort of tension in the pantomime between the real and the unreal, between the natural and the unnatural, that keeps the spectator continually off balance. It is exactly this kind of complex interplay between real and imaginary frames of reference that one finds later in *Les Mamelles de Tirésias*. The ambivalence between reality and unreality also prefigures the "quarrel" in "La Jolie Rousse" in 1918 between tradition and invention on the one hand and Order and Adventure on the other.

Since Apollinaire was the first to employ the term "surréalisme," *A quelle heure* might also be called "The First Surrealist Play." More significantly, the existence of this pantomime has important implications for the history of modern drama. Critics have occasionally claimed, for example, that *Les Mamelles de Tirésias* was merely a clever imitation of Jean Cocteau's *Parade*, which had been performed one month earlier. The discovery of *A quelle heure* effectively refutes this argument by showing that Apollinaire was writing similar plays a good three years before. It is evident that the later play owes almost nothing to Cocteau's work—as Apollinaire protested on several occasions—and that it derives instead from his dramatic experiments in 1914. While the pantomime's historical importance is undeniably great, it is a work that deserves admiration in its own right. Its history has been rather paradoxical. Originally conceived as a poem, then as a pantomime, later as a ballet, it managed to be influential despite the fact that it was never performed. Prevented first by the outbreak of World War I, then by the death of Apollinaire, it testifies nevertheless to the creative vigor of its author and to the artistic fertility of the years immediately preceding the war.

4
Alberto Savinio at Home

While *A quelle heure un train partira-t-il pour Paris?* exhibits few traces of Picabia, Savinio's presence is both abundant and pervasive. Although Raymond Pouilliart claims that the composer had no effect upon Apollinaire's art, he is almost certainly mistaken.[1] Before tackling this question, however, I will examine the professional relationship that existed between the two artists in an effort to correct a widespread error. Apollinaire's admiration for Savinio's music has often been subjected to ridicule by critics who allege that he loved the violence of the Italian's performance more than the compositions themselves. While this is far from the truth, Apollinaire certainly made no effort to dissipate this impression. Indeed he even seems at times to have encouraged it. A distinction must be made in any case between Savinio's performative mode and his musical inspiration. The violence associated with his performance, which may have been inspired by the Futurists, simply testified to the abundant creative energy with which the works were conceived. A careful reading of Apollinaire's criticism in any event reveals an interesting fact. One soon discovers that he took pleasure in deliberately exaggerating the brutality of Savinio's playing. Although this was perhaps intended as a joke, it also served to generate a little publicity for the composer. Whatever the explanation, one has great difficulty in believing statements such as:

> Et après chaque morceau on étanchait le sang qui maculait les touches.
>
> (And following each composition [there were eleven] he attempted to staunch the blood that spattered the keys.)

or

> . . . après chaque morceau de musique on enlevait les morceaux du

piano droit qu'il avait brisé pour lui en apporter un autre, qu'il brisait incontinent.

(. . . following each composition they took away the pieces of the upright piano he had broken and brought him another one, which he immediately broke as well.)[2]

On the other hand, one detects a genuine enthusiasm on Apollinaire's part for his friend's music, which he believed had great artistic potential:

Dans les *Chants de la mi-mort,* notamment . . . nous nous trouvâmes en face d'une poésie musicale si imprévue et si choquante, que nous sommes persuadés que cette oeuvre pourra constituer dèsormais le point de départ d'une orientation de la musique moderne.

(In the *Songs of Living Death* especially . . . we were confronted by a musical poetry so unexpected and so shocking that we are persuaded that this work will serve as the point of departure henceforth for a new direction in modern music.)[3]

This was high praise indeed, and Apollinaire's choice of critical language leaves no doubt that it was sincere. In the space of a single sentence he employed three key terms that were associated with his own aesthetics: "imprévue," "choquante," and "moderne." Interestingly, he was shortly to form an equally high opinion of the poems upon which the music had been based.

Various bibliographies and the composer's own testimony reveal that Savinio had long been interested in dramatic genres connected with music, such as opera and ballet. Apollinaire himself remarked that he was "un esprit éminement dramatique" ("an eminently dramatic spirit").[4] The long article that Savinio published in *Les Soirées de Paris* in April, entitled "Le Drame et la musique," described in detail the new aesthetic that he had just formulated. Its central organizing principle was that of a synthesis of the arts, which seemed more analytic than synthetic initially:

. . . j'ai la conception d'une oeuvre constituée à la fois d'éléments dramatiques et musicaux, mais où ces éléments—contrairement aux méthodes usées—ne se soutiendraient par aucune dépendance mutuelle.

(. . . my conception is of a work that is composed of dramatic and musical elements at the same time but in which these elements—

contrary to methods that have become exhausted—do not support each other by any kind of mutual interdependence.)

Thus the essence of his aesthetics consisted in the juxtaposition of disparate elements, as in Apollinaire's poetry and in much of modern art during this period. The main difference was that in Savinio's case the elements were taken from two different arts: music and drama. Apollinaire was to adopt a similar aesthetic in "Lettre-Océan" only two months later, in June 1914. Combining poetry and painting, he achieved a synthesis of two different arts that resulted in the creation of a whole series of "idéogrammes lyriques."

Writing in *Les Soirées de Paris* in May, Savinio provided additional information about his new method in a long "Note." Rejecting traditional polyphony, for example, he called for the creation of a "musique desharmonisée" from which any suggestion of harmony would be banished. Exemplifying an aesthetics of dissonance, his music was inspired by Stravinsky's compositions on the one hand and by various Futurist compositions on the other. Savinio strove to revolutionize musical structure as well by rejecting traditional forms he felt had become outmoded. "La structure se base essentiellement sur le dessin" ("My structures are based essentially on drawing"), he volunteered concerning his most recent works, which thus drew on three different artistic areas. Unfortunately, since he did not go into detail one has little idea of what was involved. Certainly music, drama, and art played a key role in his compositions, where they blended together to form an extraordinary new genre. It is also known that Savinio's music incorporated various sounds that were unrelated to the action taking place on stage. In addition the composer introduced an unrelated melody from time to time, such as a popular song or a folksong. These tunes were not chosen at random but were suggested by the preceding dramatic events. The article's most interesting section, perhaps, concerned Savinio's concept of cubist counterpoint, which called for dramatic and musical elements to function independently of each other. This is undoubtedly how *A quelle heure* itself would have been presented if the war had not prevented Savinio from implementing his radical new aesthetic.

Influences and Resemblances

As noted previously, Apollinaire attached great importance to

Les Chants de la mi-mort. It is clear that he preferred this composition to all the others by Savinio and that it made a considerable impression on him. According to the composer's own testimony, it was the only work performed at the May recital, except for *Niobé*, that embodied the criteria set forth in his article in April. This modernity, this bold new aesthetic vision, was not limited to the music in *Les Chants de la mi-mort* but encompassed its poetic and dramatic aspects as well. Fortunately, and probably in response to Apollinaire's request, Savinio published the dramatic poems in the last issue of *Les Soirées de Paris* (July–August 1914).[5] Conceived as fragments of a larger work that was never completed, they are deliberately disjointed. The project itself evolved into a novel entitled *Hermaphrodito,* which was serialized in *La Voce* in 1916 and published in 1918.[6]

Despite the undeniable originality of *Les Chants de la mi-mort*, one easily detects the influence of Giorgio de Chirico, Friedrich Nietzsche, and the Italian Futurists. In the first instance, symbols and objects from de Chirico's pictures are strewn across the work, including a tower, the masts of a three-masted sailing vessel, and an equestrian statue of a king. In the second, the "Chant de la nuit" ("Song of the Night") sung by the Bald Man at the end is modeled on a similar song in Nietzsche's *Also Sprach Zarathustra* (chapter 31). Finally, one detects numerous traces of the Futurist cult of the machine, usually with sexual overtones as in the following passage:

> Les grosses machines noires frémissent, elles entrent en action. Les roues énormes tournent vertigineusement, roulées dans les courroies de cuir; les pistons jaillissent par saccades, et replongent dans leurs étuis d'acier.
>
> (The huge black machines shiver; they begin to operate. The enormous wheels turn dizzily, revolving in pulleys made of leather; the pistons shoot forth in bursts and plunge back into their steel housing.) (P. 23)

In addition *Les Chants de la mi-mort* is indebted to Luigi Russulo's *L'Arte dei Rumori* (11 March 1913) and to Balilla Pratella's *La Musica Futurista: Manifesto tecnico,* issued on 11 May 1911. As Pratella advised, for example, Savinio is himself the author of the dramatic poems for which the music was composed. As the same authority recommended, the poems are written in free verse and enjoy a tremendous "libertà poliritimica," consisting for the most part (again according to Pratella's directions) in the contrast of several musical "motivi passionali." This contrast gives the work much of its peculiarly dadaist flavor, for Savinio likes to juxtapose several different moods ("motivi passionali"), suddenly cutting from one to the other to produce unexpected transitions.

Much of the work's dadaist flavor also comes from the astonishing characters and incredible situations with which it is concerned. Curiously, there is little humor in these poems, the author's love of the absurd manifesting itself primarily as a predilection for the grotesque. This, along with the ornate, florid language and the constant tendency toward melodrama, combines to produce a work that is somewhere between the Baroque and the Romantic. At the same time, however, *Les Chants de la mi-mort* is definitely an avant-garde phenomenon.[7] It is simply amazing how much it resembles not only *A quelle heure un train partira-t-il pour Paris?* but also *Les Mamelles de Tirésias*. For the present it suffices to note that all three plays contain bizarre characters, an abundance of surprise, a desire to shock, and great quantities of enthusiasm. All three are concerned with the universal constants of human experience, although the subtitle of Savinio's opera scarcely prepares us for this aspect: *Scènes dramatiques d'après des épisodes du Risorgimento (Dramatic Scenes Based on Episodes From The Risorgimento)*. One is reminded once again of Giorgio de Chirico's paintings that are filled with allusions to the unification of Italy.

Les Chants de la mi-mort

The first thing one discovers is that *Les Chants de la mi-mort* contains very little that corresponds to its subtitle. To be sure, we know from de Chirico's paintings that the equestrian statue in the play must depict Vittorio Emanuele II, who in 1861 became the first king in Italy.[8] Savinio commemorates this historical event a little later when an anonymous voice cries: "Vittorio Emanuele, re d'Italia!" (p. 23). But since the equestrian statue is never identified in *Les Chants de la mi-mort*, the spectator is left in ignorance as to its identity. The other allusion to the Risorgimento occurs near the beginning of the same scene where one encounters a "chant de volontaires" ("song of the volunteers"), which, contrary to the rest of the play, is written in Italian:

> Ad-dio mia bel-la, ad-di-i-o!
> l'a-armata se-e ne va (param, pam, pam),
> e se non partis-si anch'io

> sarebbe una viltà . . .
> e se non partis-si anch'io
> sarebbe una viltà.
>
> (Goodbye, my love, goodbye!
> the army is departing [param, pam, pam],
> and it would be a cowardly thing
> if I did not depart as well.)
>
> (p. 18)

Although the stanza contains remarkably little information, one gathers from the fact that it is in Italian that the scene is situated in Italy. I am grateful to Antoine Fongaro for identifying the song itself.[9] Composed by Carlo Alberto Bosi in 1848, before the battle of Curtatone, it was originally entitled "Il volontario parte per la guerra d'indipendenza" ("The Volunteer Departs for the War of Independence"). The lines cited by Savinio seem to come from the popular version that evolved subsequently and was known familiarly as "L'addio del volontario." However, *Les Chants de la mi-mort* is not really concerned with Italian history but with the psychology of the unconscious. This was an astonishing subject for Savinio to choose at such an early date, although D. H. Lawrence had published a novel *(Sons and Lovers)* on a similar theme the year before. Even more astonishingly, Savinio's psychological insights are both well-informed and profound. As André Breton has observed, Savinio's work, like that of his brother, transports the reader or spectator "au coeur même du monde sexuel symbolique" ("into the very heart of the sexual symbolic world").[10] Indeed he has analyzed the symbolism of *Les Chants de la mi-mort* so well in his *Anthologie de l'humour noir* that there is scarcely need to discuss it here. For the most part the work is an allegorical treatment of a particular family. More specifically, it dramatizes the unconscious (and ambivalent) feelings of a mother, a father, and their son when the latter decides to leave home and take a wife (or mistress). Breton emphasizes the autobiographical aspects of *Les Chants de la mi-mort* while speculating about the relationship between Savinio and his parents.

Although the work itself is extremely complex, the plot around which it is built is relatively simple. After the son and his girlfriend have spent the night together—an experience the father secretly witnesses—the lovers are discovered by the mother. The latter's arrival is in fact instigated by the father, who indignantly points to the sleeping lovers. Equipped with an electric spear, which—tellingly—she has procured from the father, the mother kills the girl and then gives vent to her grief:

> Ah! Nino! apprends donc ma souffrance.
>   (Elle hurle de rage)
> Toi, fille de putain,
> fille de femme fardée,
> tu voulais me le prendre!
>
> (Ah! My son! Hear my terrible suffering.
>   [She screams with rage]
> You, the daughter of a whore,
> the daughter of a painted woman,
> you wanted to take him from me!)
>
>   (pp. 19–20)

Upon awaking the son discovers that his girl friend is dead and loses his mind. He pounces on his mother and kills her. Then he experiences more tender emotions: "Il l'embrasse, la berce; il la lance au plafond et la rattrappe. Il la jette par terre et la piétine. Grands éclats de rire" ("He embraces her and cradles her in his arms; he tosses her up to the ceiling and catches her. He throws her on the floor and tramples on her. Great bursts of laughter") (p. 22). The play concludes with the "Chant de la nuit," a moving lament uttered by the father who is left all alone and who prepares himself for imminent death. From this brief description it is evident that *Les Chants de la mi-mort* contains a rich assortment of psychological situations. Besides maternal jealousy, which culminates in an act of vengeance, the opera dramatizes a whole series of themes generated by problems associated with sexuality. These include: the father's jealousy, which mirrors the mother's and which leads him to denounce his son; the father's conspicuous voyeurism, which is related to the theme of repressed sexuality; the son's vengeance directed against his parents, which alternates with his love for them; and the conflict between sexual satisfaction and society's approval.

As it has come down to us *Les Chants de la mi-mort* consists of a "Préface poétique" and two selections from act 3, tableau 2, which bear the titles "L'Episcope" and "Scène de la tour." Even before the opera begins the list of *dramatis personae* produces a strong feeling of *déjà vu* in the reader and spectator:

L'homme-chauve	(The Bald Man)
L'homme-jaune	(The Yellow Man)

Daisyssina	(Daisyssina)
La mère de pierre	(The Mother of Stone)
Les hommes de fer forgé	(The Men of Iron)
Deux anges	(Two angels)
Un roi fou	(A mad king)
Les hommes-cibles	(The Human Targets)
Un garçonnet	(A little boy)
Statues	(Statues)
Machines	(Machines)
Voix	(Voices)

Among other things this list suggests that Savinio's opera is affiliated with *A quelle heure un train partira-t-il pour Paris?* For one thing, the Bald Man (the father) strangely resembles the man with no eyes, no nose, and no ears in Apollinaire's pantomime. For another, the Yellow Man (the son), a Futurist character in the tradition of the Variety Theater, recalls the blue and red women who follow the musician of Saint-Merry. The family is completed by the Mother of Stone, who eventually murders Daisyssina, her son's lover. One also encounters various voices and machines that recall those in the pantomime. One wonders if Apollinaire's automatic characters resemble the latter or if they are related to the Men of Iron instead.

In addition Apollinaire's automatic sovereign could conceivably be a descendent of Savinio's mad king. To kill oneself for no reason is certainly the act of a deranged person. Whatever the explanation, chapter 5 will explore some of the differences between the two kings as well. For the moment it suffices to examine the character in *Les Chants de la mi-mort*. Like the automatic sovereign this character plays an enigmatic role and appears onstage only briefly:

VOIX DU ROI AFFOLÉ (venue du dehors)
"Ah! éteignez le phare si vous ne voulez pas me voir mourir!"
(Par l'ouverture carrée du bas de la tour pénètre le rayon circulaire d'un phare; les rayons se succèdent à intervalles réguliers.)
Entre le roi, affolé; de ses mains pâles, il presse une couronne sur sa tête; il tourne plusieurs fois autour de la statue équestre; il sort, dans une rafale soudaine.

(THE VOICE OF THE MAD KING [from afar]
"Ah! extinguish the beacon if you do not want to watch me die!"
[The square opening at the bottom of the tower is filled with a

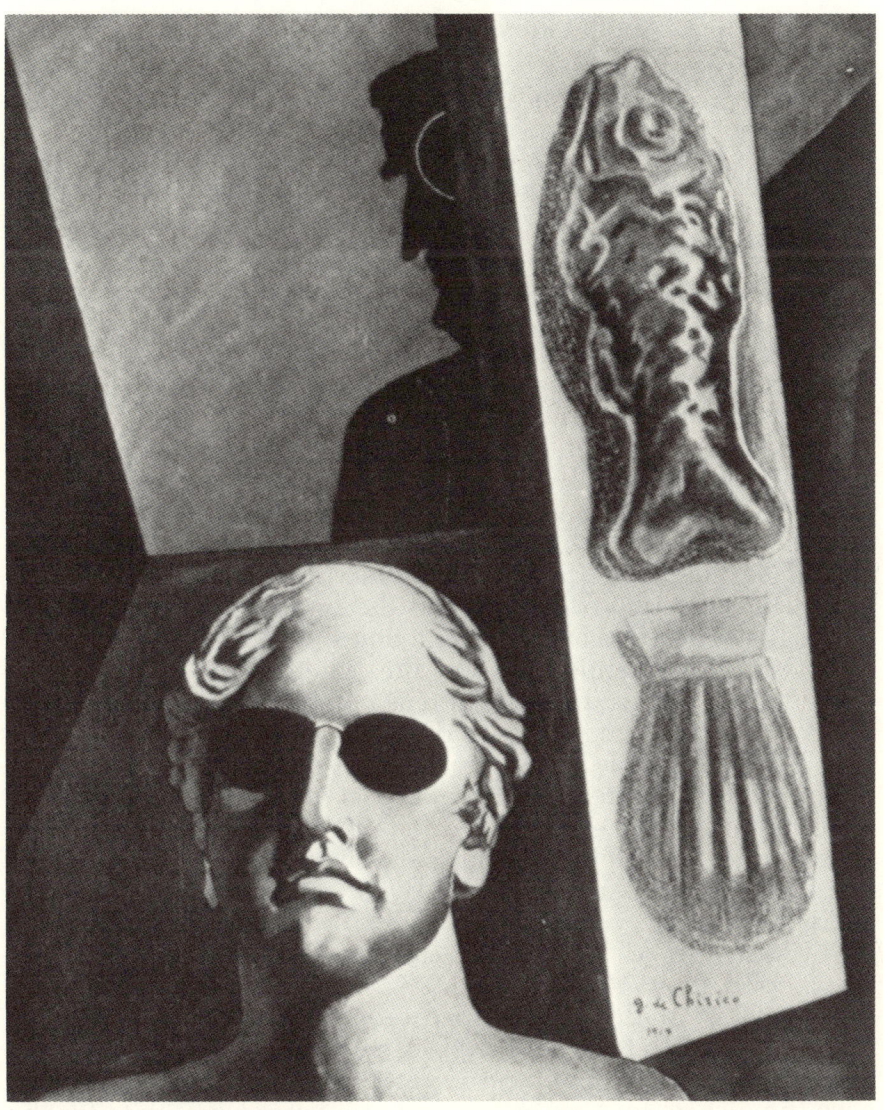

8. Giorgio de Chirico, *Portrait of Guillaume Apollinaire*, 1914. Oil on canvas. 34×27". Collection Musée National d'Art Moderne, Centre Georges Pompidou, Paris.

beacon's circular beam; the beams succeed each other at regular intervals.]

The king enters, crazed; with his pale hands he presses a crown on his head; he circles the equestrian statue several times; he leaves in a sudden squall.) (Pp. 22-23)

Despite the interpretative difficulties that this brief scene presents, readers who are familiar with Savinio's and de Chirico's symbolic language, which they shared in common, will doubtless agree as to the mad king's identity. The character in question is beyond a doubt the philosopher Friedrich Nietzsche, whom the brothers preferred to all other writers and who exerted a singular influence on their art.[11] Undermined by insanity toward the end of his career, when he was living in Turin, Nietzsche believed he was Vittorio Emanuele II.[12] In support of this interpretation it should be noted that Savinio juxtaposes this character with the Italian king on two occasions. On the one hand, the mad king circles the equestrian statue several times, which (as noted) represents Vittorio Emanuele II. On the other hand, this scene is immediately followed by the latter's coronation, represented by the cry "Vittorio Emanuele, re d'Italia." A tragic figure, like the Bald Man at the play's end, the German philosopher symbolizes the unstable, transitory, and fatal aspect of existence. Despite his uncommon genius—symbolized here by the beacon—he can escape neither insanity nor death. Announced at the beginning of the scene, death carries him away at the end disguised as a sudden squall.

The discovery of the Human Targets is as interesting as it is unexpected. In 1914, the year *Les Chants de la mi-mort* was composed, Giorgio de Chirico painted his *Portrait of Guillaume Apollinaire*, which featured the black silhouette of a human profile with a white circle drawn on its left temple (fig. 8). The painter gave the picture to Apollinaire the same year in gratitude for the praise he had received in the latter's art columns. It is doubtful, however, that the picture was originally conceived as a portrait of Apollinaire. While considerable disagreement exists on this point, those who seek to identify the silhouette with the French poet will have to resolve the following objections. In the first place, nothing in the painting recalls Apollinaire in particular. Neither the marble bust in the foreground nor the menacing silhouette in the background have more than a cursory resemblance to the author of *Alcools*. It suffices to consult a recently discovered drawing of the individual in the silhouette, which seems to represent a sinister motif, to be convinced of this fact.[13] The brooding figure portrayed in this drawing is frankly repulsive. In the second place, the silhouette occurs in at least one other painting, *The Destiny of the Poet*, which has nothing to do with Apollinaire.[14] Finally, except for a self-portrait dated 1913, living persons are conspicuously absent from de Chirico's metaphysical paintings, which are devoted to mythological characters (Ariadne) or to functional abstractions (The Philosopher). The rare portraits that do exist are invariably realistic studies. The unavoidable conclusion, therefore, is that de Chirico rebaptized the picture in Apollinaire's honor shortly before he gave it to him. As the next chapter will demonstrate, it belongs to a series of works elaborated at this time that examine the nature of lyric inspiration: *The Departure of the Poet, The Return of the Poet, The Destiny of the Poet*, and *The Portrait of the Poet*. Since Apollinaire belonged to the lyric fraternity, a stroke of the pen sufficed to transform the generic study into an individual portrait. De Chirico may also have added the white circle at this time, for reasons that will soon become apparent.

The origins of the so-called portrait were further obscured in 1916 when Apollinaire was wounded at the front. Curiously, something about the poet caused numerous myths to spring up around him during his lifetime and in the years following his death. Before long, for example, the myth arose not only that the silhouette represented Apollinaire but also that the circle marked the spot where he was destined to be wounded. People began to speak of the "portrait prémonitoire" with awe. In the excitement everyone forgot that he had been wounded in the right temple rather than the left. Apollinaire himself did nothing to dispel the rumors of de Chirico's supernatural powers. For one thing, he loved a good joke as much as anyone and delighted in the mysterious aura that accompanied the story. For another thing, well before he was wounded he used to call the silhouette "l'homme-cible" ("the human target") and claimed that it was a good likeness of himself.[15] In this he was joined by Savinio and de Chirico, who shared the same terminology and who had reasons of their own for perpetuating the myth.[16] In view of its unusual history it is no wonder that the poet developed a lasting fascination with the painting, a fascination bordering on obsession when he was sent to the front and actually became a human target. For the present purposes the most significant fact is Apollinaire's use of the term "homme-cible" to describe his "portrait." Since the composition of *Les Chants de la mi-mort* preceded the creation of de Chirico's picture (see chapter 5), the honor of having invented the term would seem to belong to Savinio. The evidence suggests that Apollinaire and de Chirico borrowed it subsequently from *Les Chants de la mi-mort*. To be sure, Savinio's Human Targets are recognizable from the fact that they wear a red heart over their left breasts rather than a white circle on their temples. Nevertheless, from this image to the concept of a rifle-range silhouette was a simple step, one that remained faithful to Savinio's original idea.

The Bald Man

At this point it is appropriate to examine the most important character in Savinio's opera: "l'homme-chauve." It is not difficult to show that this enigmatic figure in particular was modeled on Apollinaire's phallic musician. Rather than engage in complicated proofs and detailed comparisons, the following excerpts from *Les Chants de la mi-mort* should establish his identity. Savinio seems to have made little attempt to conceal his debt to Apollinaire, which is glaringly apparent.

> *L'homme-chauve,* immobile, les bras croisés sur
> la poitrine, chante gravement le "chant de la nuit":
>
> "Gens de la cité, c'est la nuit, les étoiles . . .
> Je reste, *homme sans visage,*
> avec le fardeau de ma chair flapie.
> Ah, nom d'un chien! c'est la mi-mort.
> . . . Mais donnez-moi des pleurs, donnez-moi des sanglots . . .
> Je tends la main . . ."
>
> *Homme sans voix sans yeux et sans visage,*
> fait de douleur fait de passion et fait de joie;
> il connaît tous les jeux, il fait toutes les culbutes,
> il parle tous les langages . . .
> et il attend . . .
> Le mort revient et se regarde mort;
> cet homme noir qui passe . . .
>
> (*The Bald Man,* immobile, his arms crossed on
> his chest, gravely sings the "song of the night":
> "City dwellers, it is night, the stars . . .
> I remain, *a man with no face,*
> with the burden of my weary flesh.
> Ah, son of a bitch! it's a living death.

>   ... but give me your tears, give me your sobs ...
>   I hold out my hand ..."
>
> (p. 24)

> *Man with no voice with no eyes and with no face,*
> made of pain made of passion and made of joy;
> he knows every game, he takes every tumble,
> he speaks every language ...
> and he waits ...
> The dead man returns and regards himself lying dead;
> that black man who is passing by ...)
>
> (p. 12)

Three of the phrases quoted above have been underlined in order to call attention to the protagonist's physical attributes. As one immediately perceives, he is not only completely bald but turns out to be faceless as well. Closely related to the musician of Saint-Merry, he appears essentially as seen in Apollinaire's two works. That Savinio borrowed this character from the French poet really should not surprise one. For the latter exercized a strong influence on the young composer, who was eleven years his junior. Writing in *Paris-Journal* in May 1914, Apollinaire proudly announced that "le jeune musicien, dans ses derniers ouvrages, a supprimé les divisions par mesure" ("the young musician has refused to divide his latest works into measures").[17] Paralleling Apollinaire's decision to abolish punctuation in his poetry in 1913, Savinio's act was plainly modeled on that of his French mentor. Similarly, two of the verses cited above were modeled on one of the lines in "Le Musicien de Saint-Merry." The fact that they both describe the Bald Man further underlines Savinio's debt to Apollinaire. In contrast to the original alexandrine: "Quand un homme sans yeux sans nez et sans oreilles," Savinio employed a ten-syllable line before switching to the twelve syllables of the French poem: "Homme sans voix sans yeux et sans visage / fait de douleur fait de passion et fait de joie." He even abolished the punctuation in the original version in order to retain Apollinaire's rhythm.

As curious as it seems initially, the Bald Man resembles the pantomime's protagonist more than the poem's. Like the hero of *A quelle heure* he is both faceless and voiceless—which presumably indicates that he is lacking a mouth as well. And yet he *must* have a mouth and a voice because he is able to sing. This unresolved contradiction is another characteristic that occurs in the pantomime but not in the poem. One wonders whether Savinio planned to have his protagonist sing through a rubber washer in his throat, so that he could do without a mouth. This invention would certainly have been an excellent way of resolving the problem. Given the apparent absence of a mouth in *Les Chants de la mi-mort*, the rubber washer in *A quelle heure* may well have been suggested by Savinio. It was not part of the pantomime's original version in any case but was added at a later date, apparently on the spur of the moment.

Naturally several differences exist between the Bald Man and the musician of Saint-Merry as well. Although these characters are identical from the point of view of their physical appearance, they are quite distinct from each other on the symbolic level. Judging from the "Chant de la nuit," for example, the Bald Man must be viewed as a tragic figure, the victim of an obscure destiny, whereas "l'heureux musicien" ("the happy musician") is the master of his own destiny. A sort of *poète* (or *chanteur*) *maudit*, the Bald Man is simultaneously omniscient and impotent—which explains his existential anguish. It is clear, moreover, that Apollinaire never explained the musician of Saint-Merry's symbolism to Savinio. Whereas Apollinaire's "melodieux ravisseur" ("melodious ravisher") represents Dionysos, the Devil, and the *membrum virile*, the Bald Man embodies none of thse themes but is identified with the Father. Whereas the musician functions as Apollinaire's *persona*, the Bald Man has nothing to do with Savinio, who appears on the contrary in the role of the Yellow Man.

Unexpectedly the Bald Man also turns out to have a political identity, one that dovetails with his role as paterfamilias. Although his physical appearance derives from Apollinaire's musician, symbolically he is descended from another character entirely. In 1913 Giorgio de Chirico introduced a startling new motif into his works that soon became one of his trademarks. In painting after painting one encounters the statue of a bald individual dressed in a frock coat, who is invariably depicted from the back (fig. 9). Standing on a pedestal in the middle of a public square, he seems to be addressing the city's inhabitants about some important subject. Since the square is deserted, however, the orator's passionate speech falls on deaf (or absent) ears. His fellow citizens no longer seem interested in what he has to say. While the orator's identity is difficult to ascertain, one suspects that he is one of the heroes associated with the Risorgimento. The most likely candidates include the king Carlo Alberto, his son Vittorio Emanuele II, the latter's prime minister Camillo Benso di Cavour, the general Garibaldi, and the patriot Giuseppe Mazzini.

9. Giorgio de Chirico, *The Chimney*, 1913. Oil on canvas. Collection unknown.

In the absence of any definitive clues the best candidate would appear to be Cavour, an accomplished diplomat who completed the unification of Italy in 1861. More than any other figure Cavour deserves to be called the "father of his country."[18]

The identification of the Bald Man's political role reinforces one's impression, on another level, that he is a poet as well. For in a text dating from 1915 Savinio declared: "Désormais l'artiste créateur est homme politique, redingoté, statufié" ("Henceforth the creative artist is a politician, dressed in a frock coat and changed into a statue"), and he cited the life of Dante Alighieri as a conspicuous example.[19] This means that the statue represents not only Cavour but the Poet and perhaps the Father. From a certain point of view the three characters can be seen to be identical since they symbolize (and incarnate) the creative spirit. It is important to note that Savinio identifies the statue with a politician. This description would seem to rule out Carlo Alberto, Vittorio Emanuele II, Garibaldi, and Mazzini, while confirming the identification with Cavour, who was the most important politician connected with the Risorgimento. And if further proof is needed of the statue's identity, lingering doubts are removed by a key phrase buried in Savinio's *Hermaphrodito*. Evoking an avatar of the Bald Man, the author describes his arrival in the following terms: "Entre un monsieur en redingote de ministre" ("A man enters dressed in a cabinet minister's frock coat").[20] Juxtaposed with a frock coat, the word "ministre" provides conclusive evidence that the Bald Man is Cavour.

Savinio and Apollinaire

The last two lines of the second excerpt from *Les Chants de la mi-mort*, quoted above, raise another interesting question. "Cet homme noir qui passe"—does not this figure represent Death, personified in this instance as a human silhouette? And is not the same figure to be found in the first scene of the pantomime, where one sees "the black silhouettes of the beings whom the poet does not know but whom he has the right at last to greet"? The corresponding lines in "Le Musicien de Saint-Merry" are rather ambiguous:

> At last I have the right to greet unfamiliar beings
> They pass before me and gather in the distance

While everything about them is strange
And their hope is no less strong than mine.

Once again *A quelle heure un train partira-t-il pour Paris?* helps to clarify Apollinaire's intentions in this poem. In this case it is the dramatization of the "beings" as black silhouettes that furnishes the vital clue. For, in view of the apparent symbolic meaning of Savinio's "homme noire," these beings must represent Death on the one hand and illustrious men from the past on the other. Besides the line from Savinio's poem, additional support for this interpretation comes from the *Portrait of Guillaume Apollinaire* whose black silhouette is associated with death.

That all three works are intimately related to each other has by now become perfectly obvious. While it is easier to compare them than to sort out the different influences, Apollinaire seems to have been inspired more in this instance by de Chirico than by Savinio. The evidence for this conclusion is contained in a letter written in 1915 in which Apollinaire referred to his "portrait":

... c'est une oeuvre singulière et profonde.
C'est encore un portrait ressemblant, une ombre
ou plutôt une silhouette comme on en faisait
au commencement du XIXe siècle

(... it is a singular and profound work.
It is also a realistic portrait, a shadow or
rather a silhouette like those they used to make
at the beginning of the nineteenth century.)[21]

This remark suggests that the parade of black silhouettes at the beginning of the pantomime, which in fact resembles a series of nineteenth century cutouts, derives from de Chirico's painting. Furthermore, though various shadows figure in nearly all of de Chirico's pictures before 1916, only three works contain a human silhouette: *The Destiny of the Poet*, the *Portrait of Guillaume Apollinaire*, and *Mystery and Melancholy of a Street*. All three paintings date from 1914, the year the pantomime was composed.

Other similarities exist as well between *A quelle heure* and *Les Chants de la mi-mort*. The most interesting examples occur in the section of the opera entitled "L'Episcope," much of which is reproduced below:

Avant la levée du rideau: un coup de feu, un cri; le silence ...
Le Rideau se lève. ...

L'Homme-chauve gît par terre. Des hommes-cibles en tôle sont rangés contre le mur, la place du coeur designée par un coeur rouge. Des hommes noirs en fer forgé passent en se trainant le long du mur et en grognant. On entend sans discontinuer un roulement de tambour. . . .

Du coup le bras de l'homme-chauve rejette la couverture et sa main tient une lampe qui projette une lumière terriblement vive.

On entend l'horrible bruit d'une toile écrue que l'on déchire. Aussitôt, le roulement de tambour cesse. Silence.

UNE VOIX (dans un mégaphone)

"Enfin, Monsieur Burness, voulez-vous me dire vers quel port se dirige la 'Santa-Barbara'?"

Chant de marins. Le chant de délivrance.

Bruit de ressorts déclenchés; les hommes-cibles étirent leurs bras de fer, puis rigidment, ils font des mouvements de gymnastique suédoise.

(Rideau)

(Before the curtain is raised: a shot rings out followed by a cry; silence . . .

The Curtain is raised. . . .

The Bald Man is lying on the ground. Some Human Targets dressed in sheet metal are distributed along the wall, the location of their hearts indicated by a red heart. Some black men dressed in forged iron pass by, dragging themselves along the wall and groaning. A continuous drum-roll is heard. . . .

All of a sudden the Bald Man throws off his covering and holds a lamp in his hand that projects an extremely bright light.

One hears the horrible noise of unbleached linen being torn. The drum-roll ceases immediately. Silence.

A VOICE [through a megaphone]

"At last, Mister Burness, would you like to tell me toward which port the 'Santa Barbara' is headed?"

The sailors' song. The song of deliverance.

The sound of springs being released; the Human Targets stretch their arms of iron, then perform Swedish gymnastics with rigid movements.

[Curtain] (Pp. 15–16)

The first thing that attracts one's attention is the Bald Man, whose actions are clearly symbolic. Left for dead, covered with a heavy coat like a corpse, he comes to life at the very last moment in order to liberate humanity from its bondage—whence the "chant de délivrance" addressed to the new Messiah by his subjects in gratitude for his arrival. This at least seems to be the symbolism of the miraculous lamp that projects a "lumière terriblement vive." As elsewhere in *Les Chants de la mi-mort*, Savinio appears to be referring to the Risorgimento and to the capital role played by Cavour. It is worth noting that Apollinaire was to use similar sounds in *Les Mamelles de Tirésias* in much the same way.

Other similarities between *A quelle heure* and *Les Chants de la mi-mort* deserve to be pointed out as well: the Human Targets, for example, those bizarre characters dressed in sheet metal who move with difficulty and whose arms are made of iron. From the above excerpt it appears that they served as models for Apollinaire's own automata in the pantomime. The resemblance is striking in any case. Finally, both works contain an unexpected pistol shot and an important prop: a megaphone, used to amplify certain phrases that nevertheless remain enigmatic.

But there is no need to continue the comparison, for Apollinaire and Savinio clearly exerted a certain amount of influence on each other. There are simply too many similarities to be the result of coincidence. It suffices to recall the dates of composition to reconstruct the original sequence of events. "Le Musician de Saint-Merry," for instance, was composed sometime before 15 February 1914, when it appeared in *Les Soirées de Paris*. As demonstrated in chapter 3, *Les Chants de la mi-mort* was composed between 15 May and 24 May 1914. Luigi Rognoni, who was able to consult the original document, claims that Savinio's work was finished on 16 May 1914.[22] Since he provides no documentation, however, it is not clear whether this date is taken from the manuscript itself or whether it is merely an estimate. It is important to remember, in any case, that *A quelle heure* was created in July of the same year. This means that the original path of development extended from Apollinaire's poem to the pantomime by way of *Les Chants de la mi-mort*. Partially inspired by "Le Musicien de Saint-Merry," Savinio's composition was destined to influence *A quelle heure* in turn.

5
Giorgio de Chirico among the Mannequins

If Giorgio de Chirico's name has continually appeared in connection with the works we have been discussing, this is because his relationship to these works was far from accidental. In several respects the artist can be considered a collaborator on *A quelle heure un train partira-t-il pour Paris?* and the co-author of *Les Chants de la mi-mort*. Let me backtrack for a moment, therefore, and examine de Chirico's personal and artistic relations with Apollinaire and Savinio. By exploring the different intertextual structures linking them to each other, one will be better prepared to understand the work of all three individuals. In de Chirico's case, moreover, an interesting surprise awaits us. Giorgio de Chirico first arrived in Paris in July 1911, joining his brother who had preceded him by several months.[1] Thereafter he exhibited at the Salon d'Automne in 1912 and 1913 and at the Salon des Indépendants in 1913 and 1914. When and how he met Apollinaire is difficult to say, for there are as many versions as there are people to recount them. The most plausible explanation is that Apollinaire met the painter in 1912, as the latter's wife claims, and that he encouraged him at that time to exhibit his works.[2] The details of that encounter will probably never be known. Writing in 1914, Apollinaire merely noted:

> C'est en 1912 que j'ai eu l'occasion de dire à quelques jeunes peintres comme Chagall, comme G. de Chirico: "Allez de l'avant! vous avez un talent qui vous désigne à l'attention!"
>
> (It was in 1912 that I had the occasion to tell several young painters like Chagall, like G. de Chirico: "Keep working! Your talent is bound to be recognized!")[3]

If this date is correct, as is probable, it is curious that one whole year elapsed before Apollinaire mentioned de Chirico anywhere in his writings. Perhaps he was not so enthusiastic about the latter's art as he would have one believe. In any case there is no trace of him in Apollinaire's columns until 30 October 1913. This date marked the appearance in *L'Intransigeant* of the following remarks:

> M. de Chirico expose dans son atelier, 115, rue Notre-Dame-des-Champs, une trentaine de toiles dont l'art intérieur ne doit pas nous laisser indifférent. L'art de ce jeune peintre est un art intérieur et cérébral qui n'a point de rapport avec celui des peintres qui se sont révélés ces dernières années. Il ne procède ni de Matisse, ni de Picasso; il ne vient pas des impressionnistes. Cette originalité est assez nouvelle pour qu'elle mérite d'être signalée. Les sensations très aiguës et très modernes de M. de Chirico prennent d'ordinaire une forme architecturale. Ce sont des gares ornées d'une horloge, des tours, des statues, de grandes places désertes; à l'horizon passent des trains de chemin de fer. Voici quelques titres singuliers pour ces peintures étrangement métaphysiques: l'*Enigme de l'oracle,* la *Tristesse du départ,* l'*Enigme de l'heure,* la *Solitude* et le *Sifflement de la locomotive.*
> Il faut ajouter que la couleur de M. de Chirico est trop sombre, teintes d'étangs couverts de feuilles mortes, et ces énigmes gagneraient à être présentées sous des couleurs plus riantes.
>
> (M. de Chirico has on exhibit in his studio (115, rue Notre-Dame-des-Champs) some thirty canvasses whose inner art is consistently interesting. The art of this young painter is an inner, cerebral art which has no connection with that of the painters who have been discovered during the last few years. It does not stem from Matisse or from Picasso; it does not come from the Impressionists. This originality is new enough to warrant our attention. Ordinarily the acute and very modern sensations of M. de Chirico assume an architectural form. One encounters railroad stations adorned with clocks; towers, statues, and large, deserted public squares. Railroad trains pass by on the horizon. Here are some of the peculiar titles chosen for these strangely metaphysical paintings: *The Enigma of the Oracle, The Sadness of Departure, The Enigma of the Hour, Solitude,* and *The Whistling of the Locomotive.*
> I should add that M. de Chirico's colors are too gloomy—shades of pools covered with dead leaves—and these enigmas would benefit from being presented in more cheerful colors.)[4]

While this particular article was signed, one scarcely needs to look at the signature to recognize the key concepts of Apollinaire's aesthetics. Here the crucial terms are "originalité," "nouvelle," and "moderne"—three of the most important words in his critical vocabulary. A sort of secular trinity, they determine whether a work incorporated "l'esprit nouveau," that is, whether it marked a radical new departure befitting an avant-garde creation. More than anything, Apollinaire was impressed by the originality of de Chirico's art, which, as he observed, did not resemble that of his contemporaries. Discussing de Chirico's influence on the Italian Futurists in 1918, he again focused on the painter's originality: "du reste, ce peintre d'accent si particulier est peut-être le seul peintre européen vivant qui n'ait pas subi l'influence de la jeune école française" ("Moreover, this painter has a highly personal style. He is perhaps the only living European painter who has not been influenced by the modern French School").[5] It should also be noted that the 1913 article included three key terms taken from de Chirico's own vocabulary: "métaphysique," "énigme," and "énigmatique." During this period *énigme* and its derivatives figured prominently in the titles of his paintings, in which they evoked the mystery of the human condition. On the other hand *métaphysique*, which denoted a vision of existence verging on what Apollinaire was to call the "surreal," does not appear in a title until 1916 in the Metaphysical Interior series. Various manuscripts reveal, however, that de Chirico was using the term to describe his art as early as 1911. Among other things, this means that Apollinaire took pains to acquaint himself with the artist's theories before writing the article.

Between this date and the outbreak of World War I de Chirico was mentioned some dozen times by Apollinaire, serving on 15 March 1914 as the springboard for his pronouncements concerning the importance of surprise in avant-garde aesthetics. Similarly, about the time of his first mention of de Chirico Apollinaire began to spend more and more time with the artist. Through his intermediary he undoubtedly met Alberto Savinio as well. A bit later, during 1914, Apollinaire persuaded Paul Guillaume to include de Chirico's works in the gallery he was opening.

Numerous tokens survive of the friendship and mutual esteem that existed between Apollinaire and the painter. Besides the *Portrait of Guillaume Apollinaire,* there are several other portraits of the poet: (1) a charcoal-on-paper version of the latter painting that probably dates from after 1925;[6] (2) a drawing of Apollinaire as a Greek god, apparently dating from the 1920s or 1930s;[7] and (3) *Apollinaire Citaredo* (1942), which depicts the poet playing a lyre, dressed in a toga, and wearing a crown of laurel.[8] Apollinaire in turn dedicated a poem to de Chirico ("Océan de terre") and owned several pictures by the artist. Jacqueline Apollinaire wrote to James Thrall Soby in 1950 that her husband's de Chirico collec-

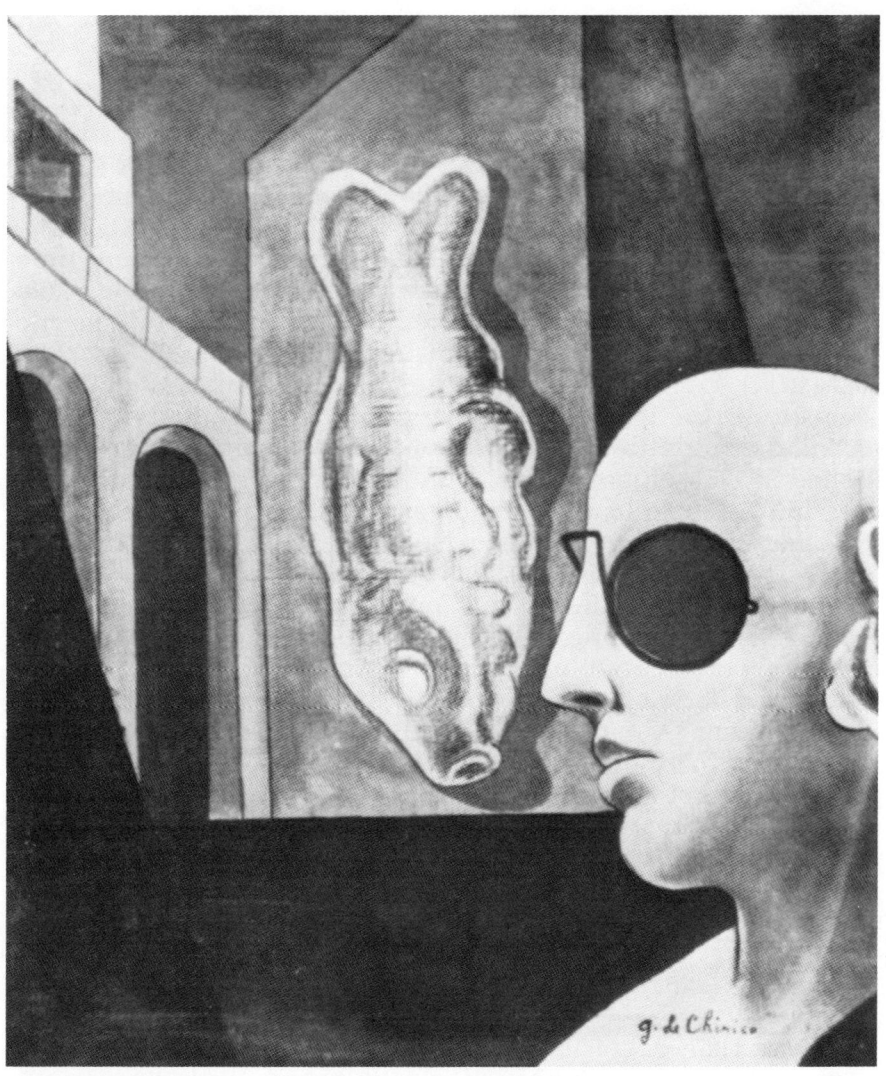

10. Giorgio de Chirico, *Portrait of the Poet*, 1914. Oil on canvas. Collection unknown.

tion consisted of two paintings in addition to the *Portrait of Guillaume Apollinaire*. One of these, she reported, was destroyed by the Germans during the Occupation. The other was sold at some unspecified time to person or persons unknown.[9] Fortunately, both the "lost" paintings are still in existence today. The collector Bernard Poissonnier seems to have acquired them from Mme. Apollinaire, who was embarrassed to admit she had sold them. The second painting was reproduced by Pierre Cailler in 1965 in his iconography of Apollinaire and is entitled *Portrait of the Poet* (1914).[10] The first painting is more difficult to identify but seems to be the work entitled *The Great Tower* (1913), which was recently acquired by the Kunstsammlung Nordrhein-Westfalen, located in Düsseldorf.[11] This is undoubtedly the picture that figured in the Apollinaire exhibition at the Bibliothèque nationale in 1969 that was formerly in his personal collection.[12] The catalogue also lists a metaphysical drawing by de Chirico (No. 437) that belonged to Apollinaire as well. Yet another myth that sprang up around the poet's name was that he supposedly collaborated with de Chirico on some of his paintings. André Breton declared, for instance, that de Chirico "avant 1917 s'est remis souvent du soin de dénommer ses tableaux à Apollinaire" ("often gave the task of naming his paintings to Apollinaire before 1917").[13] In point of fact there is not a shred of evidence to support this assertion.[14] One suspects that Breton confused the poet with de Chirico's dealer, Paul Guillaume, who in fact seems to have chosen some of the artist's titles.

From the Paintings to the Poetry

The problem of collaboration must be abandoned at this point in order to consider the question of influence, including an appraisal of Savinio's role, which was far from negligible. Indeed a complicated three-way exchange existed between the individuals in question. The situation might be diagrammed as an equilateral triangle with one person at each corner—each one influencing, and being influenced by, the other two. The relationship between Apollinaire and Alberto Savinio has already been examined in considerable detail. Concerning the de Chirico-Savinio leg of the triangle it suffices to record the intense emotional bond that existed between the two brothers. Given this tremendous attachment and the fact that they shared an apartment (with their mother) during their stay in Paris, it is not surprising that they influenced each other during this period. Together they explored the same themes, the same techniques, and the same metaphysics, while inventing a new "langage symbolique, concret, universellement intelligible" ("concrete, symbolic language that was universally intelligible"). This phrase is taken from André Breton's *Anthologie de l'humour noir,* which contains what is probably the best comparison of de Chirico's and Savinio's works. Several examples of fraternal influence will be examined later in this chapter.

As for the Apollinaire-de Chirico leg of the triangle, a good place to begin is with Scott Bates's observation in 1967 that the paintings would seem to be related to "Le Musicien de Saint-Merry."[15] The fact that the Ariadne motif was utilized by both individuals at about the same time is intriguing, to say the least. The same thing may be said of de Chirico's omnipresent dummies, which bear a certain resemblance to Apollinaire's faceless musician. With whom did these images originate, one wonders, and what paths did they take subsequently? Judging from the available evidence, they appear to have been the objects of a

11. Giorgio de Chirico, *Ariadne*, 1913. Oil on canvas. 53 × 70¾". Private Collection, U.S.A.

mutual exchange. In the first instance it seems fairly certain that Apollinaire's Ariadnes were inspired by the treatment this character received in de Chirico's works. For one thing, the poet first mentioned Ariadne in "Arbre," which was published on 10 March 1913, whereas she appeared the year before in a painting entitled *Melanconia*. For another thing, Apollinaire was relatively indifferent to Ariadne's story, employing her only once more, in "Le Musicien de Saint-Merry."

By contrast de Chirico's interest in Ariadne approached the point of obsession. In 1913 he painted no fewer than seven pictures—half his artistic production—in which a major iconographic role was played by a statue of her asleep on the island of Naxos (from which she was eventually rescued by Dionysos) (fig. 11). He even made himself a plaster statue of this character to serve as a guide in his paintings. Abandoned on Naxos by her lover Theseus while she was asleep, Ariadne serves as a poignant symbol of betrayal in love and of the loss of innocence in general. In Song 64, which recounts Ariadne's history in a leisurely fashion, Catullus speaks of the "lying sleep" that conceals the cruel truth from her. Despite the tragedy that awaits her, she will remain happy as long as she continues to dream. In this context she represents the triumph of dream over adversity, of art over life. It should be added that de Chirico's interest in Ariadne was awakened, not by Apollinaire but by Nietzsche—his favorite author—whose influence pervades his art in general. Nietzsche evokes Theseus's mistress in several texts de Chirico is known to have read, including the *Dionysos-Dithyramben*, which include a poem entitled "Klage der Ariadne" ("Ariadne's Lament") that may have been modeled on Catullus. Apollinaire appears to have borrowed this character from the painter while slightly modifying her symbolism. For him Ariadne symbolized not the inevitable melancholy of love but love that was invariably fatal. To some extent his position resembled that of Racine, who portrayed Ariadne as the victim of Venus's hatred, mourned by Phèdre in two famous verses:

> Ariane, ma soeur, de quel amour blessé
> Vous mourûtes aux bords où vous fûtes laissée!
>
> (Ariadne, my sister, wounded by a fatal love
> You expired on the shore where you were abandoned!)

In this version of the myth Ariadne remained on the island of Naxos until she finally died. Interestingly, Apollinaire knew these lines by heart. Writing to Madeleine Pagès from the front on 12 September 1915, he cited this "distique adorable" ("marvelous couplet") as an example of passionate love.[16]

If Apollinaire's Ariadnes stem from de Chirico, as is probable, "Le Musicien de Saint-Merry" and *A quelle heure* ought also to reproduce the special Nietzschean dimension of the latter's paintings. They ought to reflect Nietzsche's dichotomy between Ariadne and Dionysos, between the passive and the active, between the female and the male poles of the universe. In fact, as has been demonstrated previously, the sexual dichotomy informs both of Apollinaire's works—especially the pantomime, where it is expressed in visual terms. By this date the Eiffel Tower had become a familiar figure in his poetry, thanks to the influence of Robert Delaunay's paintings, and had acquired a frankly sexual character. In poem after poem it addressed such feminine counterparts as bridges ("Zone"), wells ("Les Fenêtres"), public squares ("Les Fenêtres"), and the famous Ferris Wheel ("Tour") erected for the Universal Exposition in 1889. And yet the pantomime is the only one of Apollinaire's works in which numerous sexual symbols are arranged in opposing ranks. This structural opposition is characteristic not of Apollinaire but of de Chirico's paintings, in which towers and other phallic objects are elevated to the status of monuments and are juxtaposed with flights of feminine arcades (fig. 11).

One of Apollinaire's monuments is particularly interesting in this regard: the Tall Factory Chimney. Except for an isolated reference in "Vendémiaire" to some factory chimneys that "engrossent les nuées" ("impregnate the clouds"), this is about the only time this image occurs in Apollinaire's work. On the other hand, beginning in 1913 and continuing well into 1914, gigantic brick factory chimneys play a prominent role in de Chirico's art, supplementing the towers and other phallic artifacts. They occur in well over a dozen works, one of which is even called *The Chimney* (1913) (fig. 9) and another of which bears the intriguing title *The Surprise* (1914). In all probability, therefore, the Tall Factory Chimney was taken directly from the painter. In turn it served as a model for the other monumental characters that embody the same principle: the Eiffel Tower, the Arc de Triomphe, and Notre Dame. In *A quelle heure*, as in de Chirico's art, the symbols' proportions serve to emphasize the sexual nature of their confrontation and, more importantly, to reaffirm the sexuality of life itself.

Although Apollinaire's pantomime follows his original poem closely, several additional borrowings from de Chirico are evident. The most obvious example appears in scene 2, where the scenario calls for a black hand printed on the wall, pointing to a sign reading "rue Aubrey-le-Boucher." This, too, is one of de Chirico's hermetic symbols, though not so important or long-lived as a number of others. Nevertheless, in several of the 1914 pictures, such as *The Destiny of a Poet* and *Still Life: Turin, Spring,* there is a large, black hand painted on a wall, pointing to some unseen object or event. The effect is that of an urgent but undecipherable command handed down from Heaven by an enigmatic God. The power of that image must have attracted Apollinaire as much as its metaphysical implications. The visual effect of a disembodied hand suspended in midair was undoubtedly as interesting as the paradox inherent in a sign whose sole function was to indicate another sign.

Bananas play a significant role in de Chirico's and Apollinaire's works as well. On the one hand, the artist painted a whole series of pictures in 1913 that featured a stalk of bananas in the foreground. On the other hand, banana merchants populate both the pantomime and the original poem. In both cases there is no mistaking the erotic symbolism associated with this fruit.

Up to this point I have refrained from discussing what is surely the most unusual example of de Chirico's influence. According to all indications the painter seems to have furnished Apollinaire with his most enigmatic character: Napoleon III. One recalls that in *A quelle heure* Napoleon III is presented alternately as the last king on earth, who dies in order to be reborn in the heart of a poet (Orpheus), and as Beelzebub, Lord of the Flies. Whereas this character appears only rarely in Apollinaire, he is one of the stars of de Chirico's metaphysical theater. André Breton suggests that Napoleon III unconsciously represented de Chirico's father—which is certainly possible.[17] Judging from de Chirico's own testimony, however, Napoleon III lends himself to several other interpretations that, although they do not conflict with Breton's version, lead in other directions. These other leads will take the inquiry into the domain of mythology, on the one hand, and of politics on the other. Both a mythic and a historical figure, Napoleon III has a "metaphysical" significance as well, like all the artist's characters. In *Hebdomeros,* for example, a fascinating novel published in 1929, de Chirico stresses Louis-Napoleon's mythological aspect:

"Et nous savons ce que cela veut dire ce démon qui ricane constamment à nos côtes; vous êtes loin de la ville . . . vous êtes assis sur

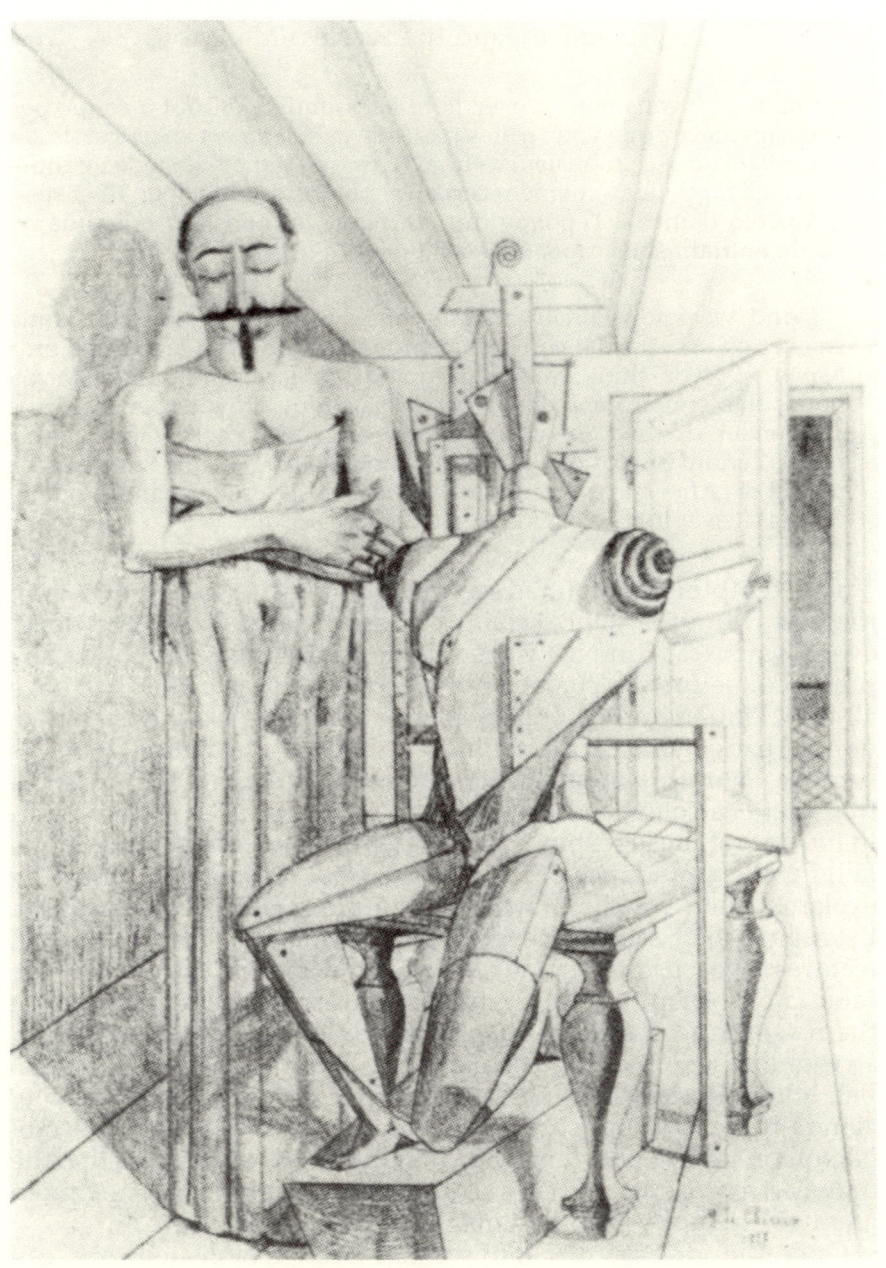

12. Giorgio de Chirico, *The Return,* 1917. Pencil drawing. Private collection, Italy.

un banc . . . vous vous croyez libre et tranquille et tout à coup vous vous apercevez que vous n'êtes pas seul; *quelqu'un* est encore assis sur votre banc; oui ce monsieur vêtu avec une élégance démodée et dont le visage rappelle vaguement certaines photos de Napoléon III et aussi d'Anatole France à l'époque du *Lys rouge,* ce monsieur qui vous regarde en riant sous cape, c'est toujours lui, le *démon tentateur.*"

("And we know what it means to have that daemon constantly snickering at our side; you are far from town . . . you are seated on a bench . . . you think you are free and at peace, and suddenly you notice that you are not alone; *someone* is sitting on your bench; yes, a gentleman dressed in old-fashioned elegance whose face vaguely recalls certain photos of Napoleon III and also of Anatole France at the period of *Le Lys rouge,* a gentleman who is observing you and laughing up his sleeve, it is he again, *the temper daemon.*")[18]

This tempter daemon, as seen in chapter 2, is none other than the god Dionysos. Once again the source seems to be the richly evocative passage in Nietzsche that describes the god's handsome presence, seductive character, and supernatural power.[19] Above all the German author depicts him as a *tempter god* whose attraction is irresistable. If de Chirico speaks of a "démon," this is because Dionysos inhabits the underworld during the winter, a trait that is also evoked in Nietzsche's text. Reappearing on earth in the spring, he is responsible for the rebirth of nature and, in the fall, for the abundance of fruits and crops. This fact undoubtedly explains why a 1917 drawing is entitled *The Return* (fig. 12). Belonging to the series devoted to the Metaphysical Interiors, it features two curious characters engaged in conversation in the middle of a room whose walls and floor are completely bare. In the foreground a strange mannequin is seated on an end table, strange because its head consists of several drafting implements. Behind it, dressed in a toga and sporting a beard and mustache, stands the god Dionysos—whose features are precisely those of Napoleon III. The fact that he has his eyes closed indicates that the drawing represents a dream sequence, an encounter occurring in another (metaphysical) dimension.

Once the identity of Dionysos has been established, one can speculate about several additional paintings. *The Joy of Return* (1915), for example, whose title recalls that of the 1917 drawing, may well have a Dionysian component. The most interesting case, however, concerns *The Child's Brain* (1914), which once belonged to André Breton. The accepted explanation of this work is that it is an imaginary portrait of the artist's father, fraught with a Freudian malaise. Thus the scarlet bookmark inserted in the yellow-brown book is usually interpreted as a symbolic reenactment of his parents' lovemaking, a scene perhaps witnessed by de Chirico as a child. Whether or not this interpretation is correct is impossible to say. But what is certain is that the man in the painting closely resembles Dionysos in *The Return*. To be sure, he is younger and has a tuft of hair on his chin instead of a long, narrow beard. Nevertheless, the mustache and frontal pose are the same, and, like the Greek god's, his eyes are closed. There is thus an excellent chance that this character represents Dionysos—a younger, more virile version than that in *The Return*. This interpretation does not conflict with previous explanations but simply adds a new dimension. As before, the subject of the work is sexual potency. If on one level the painting dramatizes the progenitive power of the Father, on another it depicts the procreative principle in general, symbolized here by Dionysos.

Before attempting to identify the second character in *The Return*, it is helpful to consider the following account by André Breton, which contains several valuable insights:

> Les fantômes . . . Si réticent qu'il se montre aujourd'hui sur ce point, Chirico avoue encore qu'il ne les a pas oubliés . . . il m'en a même nommé deux: Napoléon III et Cavour, et m'a laissé entendre qu'il avait entretenu avec eux un commerce suivi . . . l'une des dates les plus importantes à en retenir est pour Chirico celle de l'entrevue sans témoins de Napoléon III et de Cavour à Plombières. C'est, dit-il, à sa connaissance, la seule fois que deux fantômes ont pu se rencontrer *officiellement*, et de sorte que leur inimaginable délibération fût suivie d'effets réels, concrets, parfaitement objectifs.
>
> (The phantoms . . . Despite his current reticence regarding this subject, de Chirico still admits that he has not forgotten them . . . he has even named two of them for me: Napoleon III and Cavour, and has informed me that he had protracted dealings with them . . . one of the most important dates for de Chirico is that of the secret talks between Napoleon III and Cavour at Plombières. To the best of his knowledge, he says, it is the only time that two phantoms have ever met *officially*, to such an effect that their inconceivable deliberations were followed by real, concrete, and perfectly objective results.)[20]

Like Cavour, Vittorio Emanuele II, and Carlo Alberto, Napoleon III belongs to a group of historical characters associated with the Risorgimento who figure in de Chirico's paintings. In his capacity as prime minister to Vittorio Emanuele II, Cavour engaged in secret talks with the French emperor at Plombières in

July 1858. Not only did they sign a treaty of alliance between their two countries; they hatched a plot to create a kingdom of Northern Italy that eventually resulted in the country's unification. A sort of political *urszene* from which modern Italy was born, their encounter is the subject of several of de Chirico's works. This fact alone practically guarantees that the mannequin in *The Return* is Cavour. If at one level the man with the mustache represents Dionysos, at another level he is clearly Napoleon III who, as noted, was associated with the Italian diplomat in de Chirico's mind. For that matter the mannequins in general continue the symbolism of the bald statue (fig. 9), which was previously identified as Cavour.

If further confirmation is needed, one finds the same mannequin sitting on the same end table in a drawing entitled, significantly, *The Faithful Servitor* (1917). As before, drafting implements abound, but this time the figure sports a small, elongated head. Of all the heroes of the Risorgimento, only Cavour merits the appellation "faithful servitor," which describes him perfectly. A leading historian of the period summarizes his exceptional service to his king as follows: "Cavour's domestic achievements were finally overshadowed by his extraordinary triumphs in foreign policy. No ministerial career has ever been more successful than his. Having become Prime Minister when his small country was struggling to recover from the defeats of 1848–49, he died leaving his King ruler of a state five times as large, able to claim rank as one of the Great Powers."[21] Cavour's right to this title thus seems indisputable. It is interesting to note that *The Faithful Servitor* is also the title of a painting dating from 1916. One of several "claustrophobic interiors," in the words of James Thrall Soby, this work contains no mannequins at all but juxtaposes a tangled mass of picture frames and drafting tools with what appear to be six bars of soap. Although the symbolism here is obscure, to say the least, once again the subject seems to be Cavour. Unfortunately, Cavour's association with these objects is almost impossible to ascertain.

It remains to discover what de Chirico meant by "phantoms." According to his metaphysical philosophy, there exist certain elementary forces in the universe that have been embodied in rare individuals throughout the history of mankind.[22] These forces are also to be found in literature and in mythology, where they are personified by various characters. On the one hand, they are exemplified by the heroes of the Risorgimento, who succeeded in unifying their country only because they embodied a superhuman power. On the other hand, one thinks of numerous characters taken from Greek mythology: either gods (Zeus, Dionysos, Apollo) or heroes from *The Illiad* and *The Odyssey* (Hector, Andromache; Odysseus, Ariadne). Thus Napoleon III should be seen as a descendant of Dionysos in the sense that, like his predecessor, he personifies the spirit of creation. Like Dionysos he symbolizes rebirth and renewal—which is precisely the meaning of *risorgimento*. The two characters thus represent principles rather than persons. Their physical presence and their personal history are of little interest.

But if Napoleon III is a reincarnation of Dionysos, Cavour must, by this method, also be the reincarnation of someone. From what mythological or historical figure, one wonders, is he descended? Fortunately, the problem is not insoluble. The key is to be found in Savinio's description of the bald statue's symbolism: "Désormais l'artiste créateur est homme politique, redingoté, statufié." ("Henceforth the creative artist is a politician, dressed in a frock coat and changed into a statue").[23] As noted, the politician in question is Cavour, who was an accomplished diplomat and the architect of modern Italy. The same passage reveals that the creative artist is Dante Alighieri, sublime incarnation of the Poet. It will be seen in any case that de Chirico had long associated the statue with the author of *The Divine Comedy*. According to all appearances, then, Cavour must be a descendant of Dante. It is evident that, like Napoleon III and Dionysos, both figures are phantoms and that they personify the creative spirit. Thus all four characters embody the principle of creation—the principle of life itself. This in the last analysis is the subject of *The Return*, in which the artist celebrates this elementary principle by portraying a group of illustrious representatives. In reality, therefore, there are multiple conversations in *The Return* that take place at several different levels. Their relationships to each other can be schematized as follows:

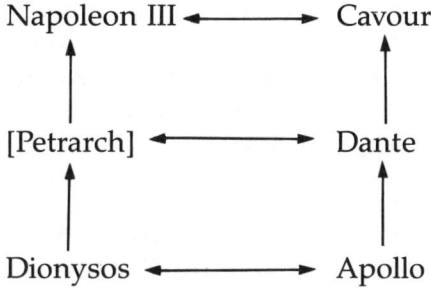

While Napoleon III and Cavour confer at one level, Dionysos and Dante are engaged in conversations with other characters at other levels. In all three cases the subject of their dialogue is the principle that animates them. Since Dionysos and Dante belong to different registers, they must be conversing not with each other but with their historical and/or mythological counterparts. Although the subject of de Chirico's symbolic system exceeds the scope of the present investigation, virtually all his paintings are governed by the ladder structure illustrated above.[24] While the Nietzschean dichotomy between Dionysos and Apollo is relatively easy to demonstrate, the identification of Dante's partner with Petrarch remains provisional at this point. Significantly, de Chirico's symbolic method recalls Dante's in several respects, as described in his letter to Can Grande della Scala, where it assumed the form of a fourfold allegory.

The mannequin figure in *The Return* also occurs in another 1917 drawing entitled *The Mathematicians* that portrays two mannequins seated face to face. Sitting on a box, the figure representing Cavour faces a personage with a large, balloon-shaped head who is seated on the now familiar end table. While there may be other conversations involved, from what has already been seen there can be little doubt that this scene is a metaphysical rendition of the conference at Plombières between Cavour and Napoleon III. The two men are "mathematicians" in the sense that they are calculating complex political strategies designed to attain several goals simultaneously. That they are the architects of modern Italy can be seen from the numerous triangles and T-squares adhering to their bodies. This explains the presence of drafting implements in the works discussed previously, especially in connection with Cavour. The fact that they replace his head in two of the drawings symbolizes Cavour's architectural mentality, his penchant for careful, meticulous planning.

Both characters in *The Mathematicians* reappear in the magnificent painting called *The Disquieting Muses* (1917). In the background one sees the Castello Estense at Ferrara, flanked by a factory with tall chimneys on the left hand and by receding arcades on the right. On the broad piazza fronting the castle, which seems to consist of wooden planking, one encounters an assortment of mannequins arranged like metaphysical chessmen. Among other things, *The Disquieting Muses* summarizes the mannequin theme since its inception in 1914. This was the last important statement of the theme in de Chirico's works, which were to become increasingly preoccupied with other subjects. With one exception all the major mannequins are assembled on the square, allowing one to trace their evolution from beginning to end. Only the mutilated mannequin of 1915 is missing—a tragic figure whose presence would be inappropriate. For while the mannequins here are meant to be "disquieting," they do not share the anguish of their mutilated brother. On the contrary, the picture possesses a remarkable tranquility. The mannequin on the left is clearly Dionysos/Petrarch/Napoleon III. If his toga-clad body is taken from *The Return*, his bulbous head, which resembles a weather balloon, is borrowed from *The Mathematicians*. The two crosses on his face are a variation of the Cretan eye motif—a symbol of the Heraclitian *daïmon*—as are the markings on the head next to the seated mannequin. The seated character is of course Cavour/Dante/Apollo, whose pose recalls any number of previous works and whose head is taken from *The Faithful Servitor*. That de Chirico juxtaposes this figure with the head of another species of mannequin may mean that they share the same symbolism. Although one can only guess at the dialogue among the various characters here, the fact that they represent "muses" suggests that, once again, the subject is creativity. While the title specifically refers to Poetry (the realm not only of Dionysos and Apollo but of Dante and Petrarch), as a political metaphor it can be applied to the creators of modern Italy. As in *The Return*, poetic inspiration combines with political inspiration to symbolize the creative impulse.

From the Poetry to the Paintings

So far I have examined de Chirico's impact on Apollinaire, but the latter's influence on the painter was equally important. Indeed it was from Apollinaire that de Chirico took the most striking of all his metaphysical inventions. At some point in 1914, probably in May or June, de Chirico began to develop a motif that would soon assume obsessive proportions and that was destined to dominate his work for the next fifteen years: the faceless mannequin. To be sure, prototypes for this character exist in the works of both men. In Apollinaire's case they go back to 1902, the date of "La Maison des morts," in which cadavers on display were compared to department-store mannequins. Nor is this an isolated instance, for another prototype appears in "L'Emigrant de Landor Road" (1904–5), together with the narrator's promise (or threat) never to return to "guider mon ombre aveugle en ces rues que j'aimais" ("guide my blind shadow through these streets that I loved"). This poem is set in a tailor's shop whose proprietor is undressing a group of mannequins, several of which have no heads. This time the comparison occurs in reverse order: the mannequins in the store's window ("mannequins victims") are compared to cadavers.

In de Chirico's case one discovers a prototype in *The Enigma of the Oracle* (1910), which features a mysterious, stoop-shouldered figure shrouded in black robes and seen from the back. This figure, which is a copy of the Odysseus in Arnold Böcklin's *Odysseus and Calypso* (1881–83), recurred sporadically in one form or another over the next seven years. In 1910 de Chirico also painted *The Enigma of an Autumn Afternoon*, which contains two important variations on the Odysseus motif: (1) a rear view of a headless, toga-clad marble statue standing on a pedestal beside a tree trunk, and (2) the statue's shadow, which is a mirror image of the Odysseus figure. One encounters the reverse of this shadow in a considerable number of subsequent works. Since it is known that the painting was inspired by the Piazza Santa Croce in Florence, the statue's source was clearly the monument to Dante that is situated in the middle of that square. At this point in de Chirico's career, therefore, Odysseus was identified in the artist's mind with the author of *The Divine Comedy* and vice versa.

Whereas the shadow soon became the most common form of the Odysseus motif, the headless statue recurred only once. Instead it underwent a startling transformation, changing into a statue of a bald-headed man in a long frock coat. This statue has already been encountered previously in connection with Savinio, where it was shown to represent Cavour on the one hand and the Poet (Dante) on the other. That this was not a totally independent invention is evident from the fact that the statue—which is again mounted on a pedestal and made of white marble—always presents its back to the viewer and has a tree trunk at its side (in one instance a fluted marble column). This bald man, who seems to possess normal anatomical features, appeared in de Chirico's pictures in 1913 and continued to appear occasionally until well into the 1920s. However, his first appearance was in a metaphysical prose poem by de Chirico entitled "La Volonté de la statue" ("The Statue's Desire"), which dates from 1912 at the latest.[25] Although the chronology of the mannequins' development is complex, the discoveries in the previous chapters permit one at last to reconstruct it. The key to the problem is contained in a study that Raffaele Carrieri devoted to de Chirico in 1942.[26] A longtime friend of both the painter and his brother, Carrieri stated that de Chirico's interest in mannequins was originally aroused by Savinio's *Les Chants de la mi-mort*. Carrieri claimed that Savinio made a sketch of the opera's protagonist—who as has been demonstrated derives from Apollinaire's musician of Saint-Merry—that immediately captivated de Chirico's imagination:

> L'origine dei manichini sta nel personaggio del dramma *I canti della mezza morte* che Alberto Savinio scrisse a Parigi e che Apollinaire pubblicò nel 1913 nelle *Soirées de Paris*. Il personaggio si chiama "l'uomo senza volto" e Savinio lo ritrasse in un disegno: "Fu il disegno del personaggio 'l'uomo senza volto' che mi ispirò l'idea dei manichini."

> (The mannequins derive from a character in the play *Les Chants de la mi-mort* which Alberto Savinio wrote in Paris and which Apollinaire published in *Les Soirées de Paris* in 1913. The character is called "the faceless man" and Savinio depicted him in a drawing: "It was the drawing of 'the faceless man' that gave me the idea of the mannequins.")[27]

Interestingly, the last phrase seems to have been uttered by de Chirico himself. Unfortunately the author neglected to document his source or to investigate the implications for the development of the mannequins. Intrigued by Carrieri's assertion, which he regarded as half supposition, James Thrall Soby asked Savinio himself about it in 1948. Savinio confirmed that Carrieri was correct, that his drawing of the faceless man ("l'homme chauve") had indeed inspired his brother's mannequins.[28] Fourteen years later, in a note he prepared for the publication of *Les Chants de la mi-mort* in *Vita dei fantasmi*, Savinio wrote: "I bozzetti dei personaggi (l'Uomo calvo e l'Uomo giallo) sono l'origine dei 'manichini' della pittura cosidetta metafisica" ("The sketches of the characters (the Bald Man and the Yellow Man) were the sources of the 'mannequins' in the so-called Metaphysical painting").[29] Ironically, no one ever seems to have asked Savinio where he got the idea of a faceless mannequin himself. And the fact that the connection between *Les Chants de la mi-mort* and "Le Musicien de Saint-Merry" has gone unnoticed has prevented scholars from seeing that de Chirico's mannequins derive ultimately, not from Savinio but from Apollinaire. Soby was skeptical of Savinio's 1948 statement and thought it unlikely that de Chirico's interest in mannequins was "merely the result of sudden literary inspiration"—although a precedent existed in the enormous influence of Nietzsche on his art.

The Mannequins

Since de Chirico subscribed to *Les Soirées de Paris*, where "Le Musicien de Saint-Merry" was published, he must certainly have read the poem when it appeared.[30] Despite this fact, the stimulus to adopt the mannequins was apparently provided not by Apollinaire's poem but by Savinio's opera. The explanation would seem to be that, unlike the poem, *Les Chants de la mi-mort* did *not* represent purely literary inspiration. On the contrary, it was largely oriented toward the aural and the visual. In addition to composing a flamboyant musical score, Savinio made extensive plans regarding the scenery and costumes. Indeed, the original version proudly proclaimed: "Décors et costumes dessinés par l'auteur" ("Scenery and costumes designed by the author"). In view of this inscription, which both explains and verifies the existence of the sketches mentioned above, it is reasonable to conclude that there existed a group of drawings by Savinio that were concerned with the opera, including additional sketches of the protagonist. It will be seen shortly that de Chirico seems to have borrowed several other motifs from these drawings as well. It is a measure of de Chirico's genius, however, that his mannequins in no way attempt either to continue Apollinaire's Beelzebub-Dionysos-*membrum virile* symbolism or to appropriate Savinio's Freudian father-symbolism. And if Cavour appears among the mannequins from time to time, one should remember that de Chirico had been interested in this character for a long time while Savinio's interest was rather recent. The same observation applies to the character of the Poet. Although the mannequins may continue de Chirico's own Dante/Odysseus motif (one painting is entitled *The Endless Voyage*), what interested him most of all was the plastic conception of the mannequin figure itself. At a time when he was searching for fresh motifs, de Chirico realized the potential of the mannequin and saw how it would fit into the metaphysical structure he had already erected. In short, he used the mannequins differently because they meant something entirely different to him.

It becomes obvious by 1915 that de Chirico had been utilizing iconographic elements from Savinio's opera for some time. Since his borrowings were limited to elements associated with the man-

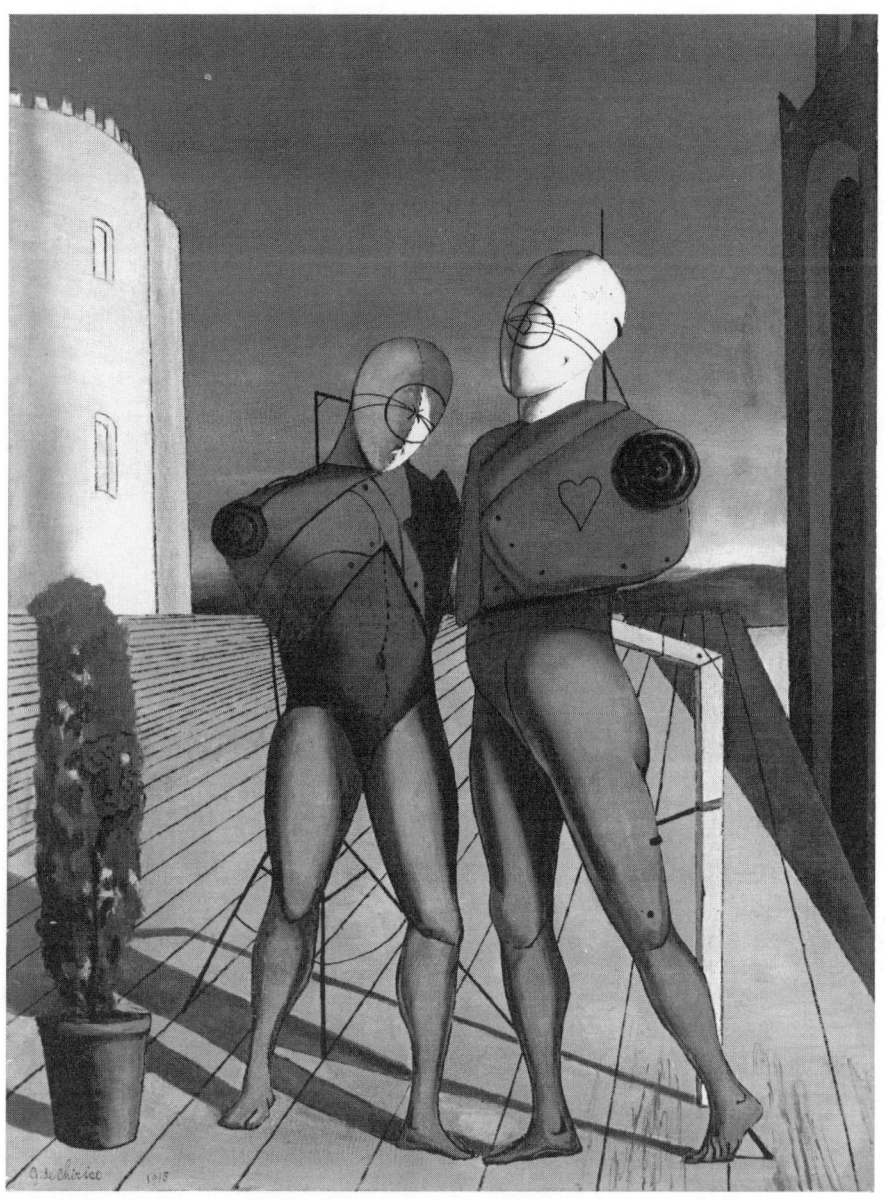

13. Giorgio de Chirico, *The Duo*, 1915. Oil on canvas, 32-1/4 × 23-1/4". Collection The Museum of Modern Art, New York. James Thrall Soby Bequest.

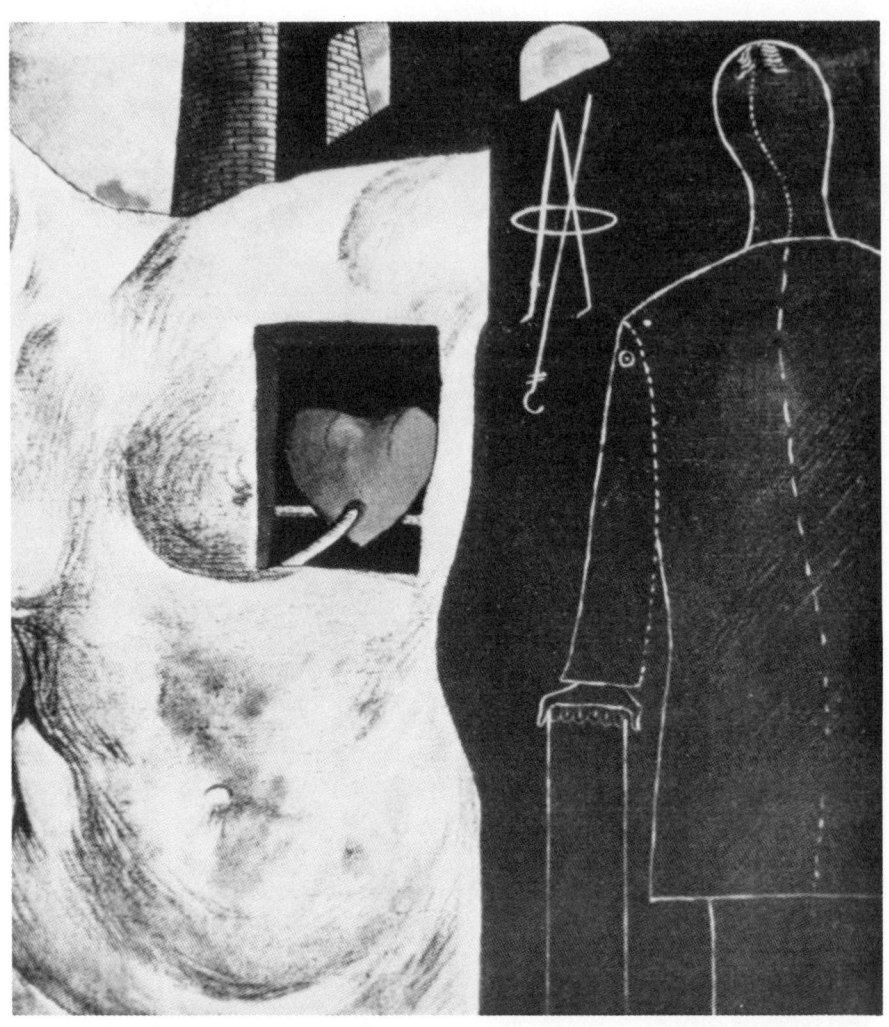

14. Giorgio de Chirico, *I'll Be There . . . The Glass Dog,* 1914. Oil on canvas. 27 × 22½". Collection unknown.

nequins, this supports the assertion that de Chirico borrowed the entire mannequin motif from his brother. I will return to the 1915 characters in a moment, but let me briefly examine the two mannequins in *The Duo* (fig. 13), which were copied wholesale from *Les Chants de la mi-mort*. Since they are dressed in sheet metal and marked with a stylized heart, they are immediately recognizable as Human Targets. Indeed Savinio's influence can be traced back through the entire mannequin sequence to the very beginning, to a painting entitled *I'll Be There . . . The Glass Dog* (fig. 14), which features a female torso from whose breast a section has been removed to reveal a stylized heart.[31] From what has just been seen there can be little doubt that this device was inspired by the Human Targets. The torso is accompanied by a rear view of a stuffed tailor's dummy, wearing a coat that has recently been assembled. Not only are the tailor's chalk marks still visible, but the seams can be seen as well. At the top of the sleeve one discovers a small circle with a point in the middle. A dotted line runs from the collar to the hem of the coat. Another follows the inside seam of the left sleeve from the shoulder to the cuff. A third line descends from the back of the figure's head to the nape of his neck.

This last marking recalls Savinio's description of how the protagonist of *A quelle heure un train partira-t-il pour Paris?* was supposed to look: "Farlo apparire con il viso imbottito di stoppa, con la cucitura che gli scendesse giù dall'occipite sino alla ganascia come una grossa vena" ("Have him appear on stage with his face stuffed with oakum and a seam running from his occiput to his jawline like a large vein") (see chapter 3). Although the intent was obviously to emphasize the phallic aspect of this personage, visually speaking the two ideas are identical. Since there is abundant evidence that *Les Chants de la mi-mort* influenced both de Chirico's mannequins and *A quelle heure*, Savinio should probably be credited with the invention of the cranial seam. There is good reason to believe that, faced with the task of translating the hero of "Le Musicien de Saint-Merry" into visual terms for his opera, Savinio chose to model him on a tailor's dummy—a logical and obvious choice. When de Chirico borrowed Savinio's faceless character subsequently for his own purposes, he perpetuated several if not all of the figure's primary characteristics. These undoubtedly included the three dotted seams in addition to the small circle.

It is evident in any case that de Chirico skillfully integrated the mannequin motif into his metaphysical iconography. He began, for example, by discreetly grafting it onto the motif of the bald

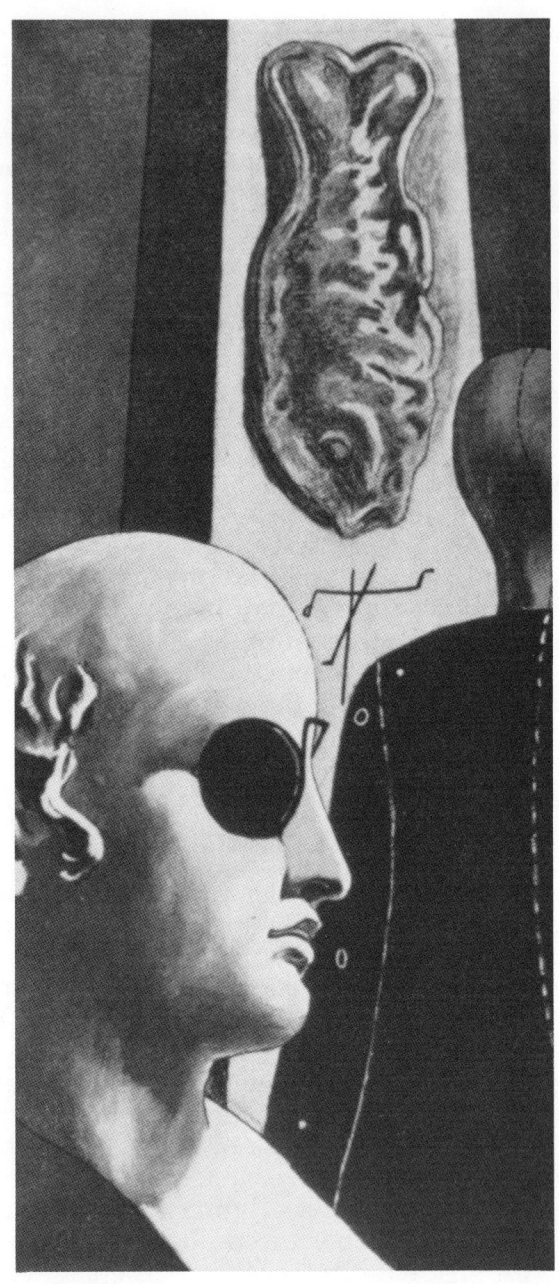

15. Giorgio de Chirico, *The Nostalgia of the Poet*, 1914. Oil on canvas. 35 × 15-3/4″. Peggy Guggenheim Collection, Venice, The Solomon R. Guggenheim Foundation, New York (Photo: Robert E. Mates). Known formerly as *The Dream of the Poet*.

16. Giorgio de Chirico, *Song of Love,* 1914. Oil on canvas, 28-3/4 × 23-3/8". Collection The Museum of Modern Art, New York. Nelson A. Rockefeller Bequest.

statue. Thus in *I'll Be There . . . The Glass Dog* the mannequin is wearing a frock coat, has his back to the viewer, and is leaning on a tree-trunk exactly like the statue of the bald man. One no longer knows whether one is looking at the statue of a mannequin or at a mannequin that is seeking to imitate a statue. The next picture, *The Nostalgia of the Poet* (fig. 15), features the same mannequin-statue hybrid (this time in a three-dimensional view) juxtaposed with the marble bust of a balding man, seen in profile like the one in *Portrait of the Poet* (fig. 10). This bust, which also appears in the *Portrait of Guillaume Apollinaire* (fig. 8), could conceivably represent a frontal view of the bald statue, whose face has always been turned away. Not only does it resemble the bust of the Apollo Belvedere in *Song of Love* (fig. 16), however, but the painting's title indicates that it also depicts a poet. In all three pictures the figure is masked by a pair of dark glasses whose function seems to be to symbolize his blindness but that give him instead the appearance of a *voyant*. Placed in the foreground where he dominates the entire composition, he appears to be addressing the viewer.

This impression is reinforced in the *Portrait of Guillaume Apollinaire*, where the bust is presented in a full frontal view. In this painting the glasses seem to conceal a penetrating gaze able to divine our innermost thoughts. Clearly this is an archetypal image of the Poet, who is endowed with the blindness of a Homer or a Milton and the clairvoyance of a Blake or a Rimbaud. It has been seen previously that the silhouette in the background symbolizes Death. The picture thus presents the Poet as a visionary and prophet seeking to interpret human experience against a background of death, which threatens to seize him—or the viewer—at any moment. To complicate matters further, the middle ground is occupied by a large fish, which is juxtaposed with an equally large scallop shell. More precisely, these objects are aspic molds that the artist has given monumental proportions. Although their function seems enigmatic, one eventually comes to realize that they serve as sexual symbols. Once again the viewer encounters the sexual dichotomy evoked so frequently by de Chirico in his works. A traditional symbol for the male organ, the fish represents the masculine principle. A traditional symbol for the female organ, the scallop shell symbolizes the feminine principle.[32] One need only recall Botticelli's *Birth of Venus*, which depicts the goddess standing on exactly the same kind of shell. Thus potency is juxtaposed with fertility and fecundation with birth. If these two principles are commonly opposed to each other, they are united here in a single, miraculous being: the Poet. A sort of

17. Giorgio de Chirico, *The Torment of the Poet*, 1914. Oil on canvas, 20-3/4 × 16-1/8". Collection Yale University Art Gallery, New Haven, Connecticut. Bequest of Kay Sage Tanguy.

18. Giorgio de Chirico, *The Endless Voyage*, 1914. Oil on canvas, 35 × 15-7/8". Wadsworth Atheneum, Hartford, Connecticut. The Philip L. Goodwin Collection.

hermaphrodite (whence the title of Savinio's book, *Hermaphrodito*), the Poet possesses the ability both to impregnate and to give birth—which capacity leads to the creation of the work of art. Parenthetically, the silhouette's dotted seam and the small circle on its sleeve prove that the picture was painted following the completion of *Les Chants de la mi mort*.

Shortly thereafter de Chirico produced his first true mannequin paintings: *The Torment of the Poet* (fig. 17) and *The Endless Voyage* (fig. 18). If the identity of the first mannequin, which is feminine, is unknown, it is clear from the title that de Chirico continued to be interested in the Poet. This impression is reinforced by the second painting, which presents the Poet in his role as Explorer and which evokes the image of a perpetual voyage—clearly a metaphor for the creative spirit ceaselessly seeking to renew itself. It is a cerebral voyage, therefore, during which the Poet continually seeks new countries, new domains to explore.[33] Among other things this theme is illustrated by the bust of the Apollo Belvedere, lying on its back, whose eyes rolled inward indicate that he is lost in poetic revery. Both works feature a frontal view of an armless, toga-clad mannequin whose arm stumps are covered by metallic cones. In addition the figure's featureless face sports what Soby calls "the black outline of a single-eyed mask" but what André Breton thinks represents a scar.[34] The metallic cones, which resemble the breastplates supposedly worn by Viking women, were quickly to become a standard part of the mannequin costume. Like the arm stumps they cover, the cones were invented by Savinio and are closely connected to the most important character in *Les Chants de la mi-mort*: the Bald Man. At the beginning of the opera, for example, Savinio provides the following description of his protagonist:

> Non! . . . Et ses moignons sans doigts
> —informes cônes de chair—
> tout comme ses pieds pointus
> sont froids . . .
>
> (No! . . . And his fingerless stumps
> —formless cones of flesh—
> are cold
> like his pointed feet . . .)
>
> ("Préface poétique," 53–56)

While the symbolism in this passage is obscure, the net effect contributes to Savinio's characterization of this figure as helpless and pitiful. In any case the cones are an excellent example of an iconographic element originally associated with the Bald Man that was taken over by de Chirico when he appropriated this personage.

The Mask-Scar

Ranking among the most enigmatic of de Chirico's emblems, the mask-scar is even more bizarre than the cones but seems to symbolize the mannequins' mute condition. It consists of a black circle situated at mouth level and held in place by two black bands encircling the head. Like the cranial seam, this also recalls a curious characteristic of the protagonist of Apollinaire's pantomime. At the last moment, the author appended a note to his scenario in which he added another dimension to his hero:

> He has no mouth but plays the flute through an opening in his throat covered by a rubber or metal washer, like those applied to horses following surgery on their respiratory tracts. (Scene 3)

MR. T. W. GOWING'S TRACHEOTOMY TUBE.

A. The cannula, with a shifting shield, armed with the pointed trochar.
B. The trochar withdrawn from the cannula, showing its peculiar construction.
C. The cannula fitted into the horse's trachea, showing how the moveable shield may be adapted, by means of a screw, to the size of the horse, or the swollen condition of the parts.

It is important to note that this device was almost certainly held in place—like most veterinary tracheotomy tubes—by cloth bands tied around the man's neck (fig. 19). In turn this suggests that the "rondelle" ("washer") and the mask-scar marking are closely related, for the resemblance between them is quite strong. They both look the same, they are both connected with mannequins, they are both located in approximately the same area, and they both came into being at about the same time.

The explanation is undoubtedly the same as for the three dotted seams: Savinio's original drawings for *Les Chants de la mi-mort* must have included this circular emblem, which Apollinaire and de Chirico borrowed subsequently independently of each other. It is reasonable to expect that, after exploring the idea of a tailor's dummy, Savinio would have modified it to include the concept of a man who was able to sing "with no voice." The rubber washer, placed either on the figure's throat or over his mouth, would have been an excellent symbol of this paradoxical ability. For it is at one and the same time a mouth *mask* and an artificial *mouth*. Although these two functions appear to be contradictory, both are related to the mannequins' muteness, which may be either inherent or induced. Indeed de Chirico may well have been attracted by the marking's ambiguity, since the "contradictory" symbolism of the rubber washer exactly parallels that of the dark glasses on the bust. While both devices appear to indicate physical limitations, in actuality they point to superhuman abilities. In every sense of the term they serve as metaphysical emblems. Whereas de Chirico previously celebrated the Poet's superhuman vision, he shifted his attention subsequently to his superhuman voice. Endowed with a prophetic ability, the Poet's words are far superior to ordinary language—what Mallarmé referred to as "les mots de la tribu" ("the words of the tribe").

It is tempting to analyze *The Torment of the Poet* and *The Endless Voyage* as anguished commentaries on World War I. Various mythological or allegorical interpretations come readily to mind, but these works almost certainly date from before the outbreak of hostilities. During 1915, however, the mannequins underwent tremendous transformations in response to the events that were taking place. De Chirico became fascinated in particular with wigmakers' mannequins, whose cardboard busts were cut away to reveal a hollow interior. His mannequins from this period have huge holes carved into their heads and bodies, as if they were the patients of a lunatic surgeon. The theme of mutilation, which is quite widespread at this time, reflects the horrors of the war. In

20. Giorgio de Chirico, *The Two Sisters,* 1915. Oil on canvas, 26 × 17″. Collection Kunstsammlung Nordrhein-Westfalen, Düsseldorf.

May 1915 de Chirico gained some first hand experience when he joined the Italian army, which entered the fray on the side of the Allies. Having usurped the role of the marble busts, which belonged to a more peaceful era, the wartime mannequins rapidly acquired an existential cast. As before, they continued to observe the human condition in their customary role as supernatural spectators, but their air of detachment was replaced by acute anxiety. De Chirico's most important inventions were the mechanical mannequins, mentioned previously, which were to alternate and combine with the stuffed mannequins as long as the motif endured. Borrowed from *Les Chants de la mi-mort*, these new characters were divided into two groups: the Human Targets (fig. 13) and the Men of Iron (fig. 21). In most cases their costume consisted of plates of sheet metal riveted together like medieval armor. In place of their arms, which were lacking, they wore metallic cones at the ends of their shoulders. In addition, as several cut-away views reveal, the Men of Iron were filled with springs and other mechanical contrivances.

The mask-scar motif underwent an almost unlimited series of transformations whose scope and complexity can only be hinted at here. Although it was still located at mouth level in *The Duo* (fig. 13), in every other instance, and as long as it continued to exist, the marking was situated at the level of the eyes.[35] Not surprisingly, its original identification with the mouth was abandoned as well. Instead the marking's new location served to restore the mannequins' (and the Poet's) visionary character, as titles such as *The Prophecy of the Scholar* and *The Seer* attest. In its original *rondelle*-double-band form, the marking did not survive 1915 but assumed several new configurations. In what was perhaps his most significant experiment that year, de Chirico decomposed the marking into two overlapping, elongated ovals (fig. 20). These were then superimposed and rotated in opposite directions to produce an X-shaped marking. *The Prophecy of the Scholar* contains the best illustration of this procedure, but it occurs in *The Vexations of the Thinker* (fig. 21) as well.

By 1917, in paintings such as *Hector and Andromache* (fig. 23) and *Troubador* the lower halves of these ovals were extended to form a new set of bands that again encircled the mannequin's head, while the top halves had atrophied slightly to become a pair of eyes. In contrast to the 1915–16 mannequins their 1917 brethren were relatively subdued. Not only was the theme of mutilation absent but love and poetry were reintroduced in the person of the troubador. In the case of *Hector and Andromache* the artist was even

21. Giorgio de Chirico, *The Vexations of the Thinker*, 1915. Oil on canvas, 18-1/4 × 15". Collection San Francisco Museum of Modern Art. Templeton Crocker Fund. Purchase.

22. Giorgio de Chirico, *The Seer*, 1915. Oil on canvas, 35-1/2 × 27-1/2". Collection The Museum of Modern Art, New York. James Thrall Soby Bequest.

23. Giorgio de Chirico, *Hector and Andromache,* 1917. Oil on canvas. Private collection, Germany.

able to introduce the love theme into the context of the war. For reasons that remain obscure, he apparently felt the crisis was over. His fears appeased at last, de Chirico was free to devote himself to a new subject that he had discovered in 1916—the Metaphysical Interiors. An eminently static subject reflecting the painter's spiritual calm, it gradually replaced the mannequin in his art.

6
The Dawn of a New Age

Marius de Zayas

As Apollinaire recognized in his poem "La Petite Auto," the declaration of war in 1914 marked the end of one era and the beginning of another. And yet the innovations associated with the Belle Epoque were destined not to disappear but to be transformed into new forms by succeeding generations. This at any rate is what occurred to the mannequin motif, which underwent a whole series of modifications according to the demands of one school or another. Although the history of this evolution exceeds the scope of the present study, it is instructive to examine the consequence of the collaboration on *A quelle heure un train partira-t-il pour Paris?* Judging from his letters to Alfred Stieglitz, for example, Marius de Zayas returned to New York in September 1914 full of enthusiasm for the experiments he had witnessed in Paris, especially those associated with *Les Soirées de Paris*. He was determined to continue those experiments in America and to introduce them to the American avant-garde. His plans, which called for establishing both an art gallery and a literary journal, bore fruit the following year. In October 1915 he opened the Modern Gallery, a venture that was patterned on French galleries such as Paul Guillaume's and Kahnweiler's and that, unlike the "291" enterprise, was frankly commercial. Similarly, in March 1915 he published the first issue of an avant-garde magazine called *291*, which was modeled on the review directed by Apollinaire. Throughout its brief existence the journal was to draw its literary inspiration from the French poet and its artistic inspiration from Picabia.

The poetry that appeared in *291*, which lasted until February 1916, was composed according to simultanist precepts that had been formulated previously in Paris. Thus the very first issue included an explanation of simultanism by de Zayas that was based on Apollinaire's article "Simultanisme-Librettisme," published in *Les Soirées de Paris* on 15 June 1914. Appearing in the initial issue of *291*, this article served as a manifesto and indicated the direction that the review would take. To illustrate his discussion of simultanism, de Zayas also included a *poème-conversation*—a genre invented by Apollinaire—of his own composition. Entitled "At the Arden Gallery, 599 Fifth Avenue," it consisted of phrases supposedly recorded at that location. But the most exciting contribution was a calligram by Apollinaire entitled "Voyage." The poem itself, referred to here as an "ideogram," seems to have been reproduced by a process such as photoengraving, for it was identical to the original version published in the last issue of *Les Soirées de Paris*. In reality "Voyage" was composed of three semi-autonomous calligrams: a cloud and a bird were positioned above a magnificent locomotive. These in turn were held together by the themes of travel, communication, and disappointment in love. The review itself consisted of a long piece of paper folded into thirds to form a sort of triptych. Significantly, de Zayas chose to give Apollinaire's poem the place of honor—the center of the triptych. In this setting it created a striking impression and illustrated the new aesthetics.

While the influence of Apollinaire's simultaneous poetry was evident throughout *291*, his figurative poetry was equally pervasive. References to Apollinaire's "Lettre-Océan" were particularly common, and one issue even included the appraisal that de Zayas had previously sent to Stieglitz. "Apollinaire, that profound observer of the superficial," he wrote, "brought to artistic significance the squeaking of the 'new shoes of the poet.' "[1] De Zayas was alluding to the section of "Lettre-Océan" in which the Eiffel Tower broadcasts several Parisian sounds, including the "creak, creak, creak" of the shoes Apollinaire had recently purchased.

The second issue of *291* (April 1915) continued the experiments that were initiated in the first. Combining visual and verbal simultanism, "Mental Reactions" was both a text and a drawing.[2] The former was a *poème simultané* by Agnes Ernst Meyer that juxtaposed her reflections with her physical surroundings. The latter was an abstract composition by de Zayas, who illustrated and interpreted the poem at the same time. Part of it was modeled on Apollinaire's calligram in the shape of a pocketwatch in "La Cravate et la montre." Another section, consisting of adroit typographical imitations of perfume labels, was suggested by a line from "Le Musicien de Saint-Merry": "Rivalise donc poète avec les étiquettes des parfumeurs" ("So emulate oh poet the labels of perfume-makers"). For that matter the general format probably derived from Apollinaire as well, who advised poets in "Zone" to imitate posters and handbills.

The next issue contained a triple collaboration on a visual poem. Agnes Ernst Meyer and Katharine Rhoades contributed the verbal elements, while de Zayas furnished the drawing. The most interesting poem, however, was to be found on the last page beneath the reference to "Lettre-Océan" cited earlier. Entitled "A Bunch of Keys" and composed by J. B. Kerfoot, it was visibly inspired by "Lettre-Océan," which poem contained three separate calligrams: a postcard, a telegraphic message broadcast in concentric waves, and a keyring.[3] A visual composition as well, Kerfoot's poem reproduced the last image while adding a witty element lacking in the original. In contrast to Apollinaire, who evoked a political demonstration in his poem, Kerfoot described the rewards of a comfortable bourgeois existence. The phrases themselves were arranged as follows: (the chain) "On this chain hangs the ring"—(the ring) "Round which runs my life"—(the keys) "Frontdoor key," "[Ci]gar humidor," "Winecellar door," "My office desk," "Safe deposit box," and—archly—"Don't you wish you knew?" Like Apollinaire's visual poetry, this clever little poem defined the boundaries of its author's existence. His was a life that revolved about the office and the home and that was characterized by repetitive indulgence in good cigars, fine wines, expensive items such as jewelry, and sex. Moreover, it was an existence to which Kerfoot was *chained* by his physical appetites.

Other examples could be cited to illustrate Apollinaire's impact on *291*, but the general pattern is clear. In addition to the review's influence in America, which was considerable, it was to generate another review, *391*, founded by Picabia in Barcelona in 1917. As its title indicates, Picabia's journal sought to continue the experiments performed by *291*, which itself had been inspired by *Les Soirées de Paris*. Adopting the format of its predecessors, it was devoted to typographical experiments and to various combinations of verbal and visual elements. Quickly becoming one of the most important Dada reviews, it exerted considerable influence on the new movement and thus on modern literature in general.

Alberto Savinio

Like his brother, Alberto Savinio remained in Paris after war was declared. Among other things he collaborated on *291* on two occasions and was planning to give a series of concerts in the

United States with Marius de Zayas and André Tridon as his managers.[4] He was undoubtedly prevented from carrying out this project by Italy's decision to enter the war. In any case he does not seem to have visited America during the war, as Michel Sanouillet claims.[5] At least no trace of such a voyage exists, and Savinio himself makes no mention of it in his numerous writings. Among his contributions to *291* a score entitled "Bellovées fatales No. 12" ("Fatal Bellowings No. 12") appeared in April 1915. Similarly Savinio published a piece of music criticism in the June issue, "Dammi l'anatema, cosa lasciva" ("Strike Me with Anathema, a Lascivious Thing"), which, despite its title, was written in French. As the title suggests, Savinio adopted a bold new revolutionary program in this article. Henceforth, he proclaimed, the artist would live an isolated existence, separated from the public by the bottomless abyss created by the average individual's lack of comprehension and preoccupation with material goods. Exiled on earth, anathematized by the multitude, he would receive their mockery with pleasure as the mark of his superiority. In several respects, Savinio's attitude recalled the *poètes maudits* of the previous century, who, like Baudelaire's albatross, felt themselves "exilé[s] sur le sol au milieu des huées" ("exiled on earth and surrounded by jeers"). In Savinio's text, however, the artist was less the victim of society than a rebel against society. Wreaking havoc on bourgeois values, he sought to become even more incomprehensible. Accordingly, part of the article was written in praise of nonsense, which represented the ultimate act of defiance.

> Le non-sens se tient en prodigieux équilibre. Il est l'expression du sentiment naturel et supérieur—vrai partout—qui a des racines dans la terre et qui s'exhausse au-delà du septième ciel.
> C'est lá que flotte la musique.
> Toute une création nouvelle est mise en mouvement,
> or tout est *chanteur*.
> Plus de doutes charmants, mais la réalité terrible et frémissante . . .
> Désormais le non-sens sera un domaine ouvert à toutes les imbécilités. Je me console: il y reste des enclos où certains gens n'enteront quand même jamais.

> (Nonsense maintains a prodigious balance. It is the expression of a natural and superior feeling—true everywhere—which has its roots in the earth and which rises beyond the seventh heaven.
> It is here that music soars.
> An entire new creation begins to take shape; now everything *sings out*.

No more charming doubts but the terrible shudders of reality . . .
Henceforth the domain of nonsense will be open to every imbecility. Even so, I console myself with the thought that there will always be some areas that certain people cannot enter.)

The aesthetics of nonsense, of course, were soon to be cultivated by the Dada movement that coalesced around this very principle. Like Savinio, the Dadaists strove to express the "réalité terrible et frémissante" of the First World War by celebrating the unreasonable, the irrational, and the absurd.

In May 1915 Italy finally entered the war, and Savinio and his brother volunteered for the army. Assigned to an office in Ferrara, they were able to continue living with their mother, who rented an apartment there. During 1916 Savinio published a few articles in *La Voce* and a metaphysical novel, *Hermaphrodito*. Interestingly, the second chapter of this work, entitled "Drame de la ville méridienne," featured a character who was descended from Savinio's Bald Man:

> Entre un monsieur en redingote de ministre. A la place de la tête, qui lui manque, il porte un petit drapeau planté sur une antenne d'acier. Il a trois jambes rigides, inarticulées, inflexibles, comme les barres d'un trépied photographique. Il patine sur des roulettes métalliques, qui grincent horriblement.

> (A man enters dressed in a cabinet minister's frock coat. In place of his head, which is missing, he wears a small flag planted like a steel antenna. He has three rigid legs, which are inflexible and unarticulated like the legs of a photographer's tripod. He is wearing metal roller skates which make a horrible grinding noise when he moves.)[6]

Like de Chirico's mannequins, this character had greatly evolved since 1914 and no longer resembled the hero of *Les Chants de la mi-mort*. Instead of the tailor's dummies, stuffed with rags and bursting at the seams, Savinio introduced a mechanical mannequin that had no head. Despite his curious physical appearance, the latter prolonged the symbolism that had been associated with the Bald Man. By the fact that he is wearing a cabinet minister's frock coat, for example, one knows he represents Cavour. In addition, this mannequin possesses some extraordinary talents. Although he has no head he is able to sing, which recalls both the Bald Man and the hero of *A quelle heure*. And despite his mechanical appearance, which suggests that he is some kind of robot, one quickly perceives that he has a human torso. Standing in the middle of the stage, he unbuttons his coat and shows the audience his internal organs. Rummaging around in his lungs, he eventually takes out an enormous heart, which he nails to a marble plaque. As noted in the preceding chapter, mutilated mannequins also appear in de Chirico's art at this time, where the theme of mutilation testifies to his personal anguish. The fact that the lower part of the mannequin's body resembles a "trépied photographique" suggests that, like the artist's own characters, Savinio's figure is an observer of the human condition.

Thereafter, in 1917, Savinio was sent to fight in Macedonia, where he remained for the duration of the war.[7] Although the date of his departure is unknown, it could not have been before June.[8] Savinio appears to have begun corresponding with Tristan Tzara in 1916, Paul Guillaume probably serving as his intermediary, as he had for de Zayas and for Apollinaire. In any event, the first issue of *Dada* (July 1917) contained an article entitled "Un vomissement musical" ("Musical Vomit") that left no doubt as to his feelings about traditional music. He did not write for this review again until December 1918 (*Dada* 3), when he published a Dada manifesto. Between the war's end and his death in 1952 Savinio wrote a large number of works. During the 1920s, moreover, he began to paint and draw professionally in the same metaphysical style as his brother. It is worth noting that several critics have called attention to the influence that Apollinaire exerted on Savinio's prose works (and those of his brother).[9] The fact that their first compositions date from the period of the collaboration on *A quelle heure* leads Orio Vergani to conclude that Savinio "era diventato, intanto, scrittore per aver conosciuto Guillaume Apollinaire" ("became a writer as a result of having known Guillaume Apollinaire").[10] This influence is especially noticeable in Savinio's humor, which he shares with Apollinaire and with Picabia. One suspects that this was André Breton's opinion as well, for all three authors are included in his *Anthologie de l'humour noir*.

Writing in 1946, Savinio declared that he had influenced the French poet himself toward the end of his life. Rereading *Calligrammes* for the first time in a while, he was struck by the familiar appearance of "La Jolie Rousse":

> Il senso in molte parti di questa poesia, e nonché il senso ma il movimento stesso e alcuni atteggiamenti sono quelli medisimi dei *Chants de la mi-mort*, da me scritti nel 1914 e che nell'agosto di questo stesso anno Apollinaire mi pubblicò nelle *Soirées de Paris*. . . .

È una gioia invece, profonda, profondissima. Gioia per un conchiuso patto di amicizia. Perché io ho pensato, ho sentito "come" la mia poesia, cioè a dire io stesso sono entrato per mezzo della mia poesia in lui, e come sono diventato lui, ossia "sua" poesia. Gioia di sentire questa reciprocità, questo legame; e che anche lui deve qualcosa a me, che a lui devo tanto.

(Quite often in this poem the sense, and not just the sense but the movement itself and some of the attitudes, are the same as in *Les Chants de la mi-mort*, which I composed in 1914 and which Apollinaire published in *Les Soirées de Paris* in August of the same year. . . .

I feel a profound, an extremely profound joy as a result—the joy produced by a pact of friendship. Because I have thought, I have felt how my poems and how myself became part of him; this is to say how I was absorbed by him through my poems. The joy of feeling this reciprocity, this bond; and that he also owed something to me, to me who owe him so much myself.)[11]

The influence that Savinio believed he saw and that filled him with so much joy unfortunately seems rather doubtful. There are, nevertheless, several similarities between the two poems, one of which is particularly interesting. It concerns a passage at the very end of the "Scène de la tour" in which the Bald Man delivers his final soliloquy:

"Or quittons-nous en silence, mon âme . . . courage!
Adieu . . . les sources se sont tues.
Moi aussi, je suis un ange mort.
Gens de la cité, c'est la nuit, les étoiles.
Je suis seul:
méfiant mais vaincu je m'abandonne sans forces
aux mains terribles et douces . . .
Ayez pitié de moi!"

("So let us part in silence, my soul . . . courage!
Goodbye . . . the springs have fallen silent.
I too am a dead angel.
City-dwellers, it is night, the stars.
I am alone:
scornful but vanquished I abandon myself weakly
to those hands, so terrible and so soft . . .
Take pity on me!")[12]

Here, in turn, is the last part of "La Jolie Rousse," which is similar in certain respects to the Bald Man's final words:

Pitié pour nous qui combattons toujours aux frontières
De l'illimité et de l'avenir
Pitié pour nos erreurs pitié pour nos péchés
Voici que vient l'été la saison violente
Et ma jeunesse est morte ainsi que le printemps . . .
Mais riez riez de moi
Hommes de partout surtout gens d'ici
Car il y a tant de choses que je n'ose vous dire
Tant de choses que vous ne me laisseriez pas dire
Ayez pitié de moi

(Pity us who are locked in continual combat
On the future's limitless fronteers
Pity us for our mistakes pity us for our sins
Now the summer arrives the violent season
And my youth is as dead as the springtime . . .
So laugh laugh at me
Men from all parts especially my fellow citizens
For there are so many things I do not dare speak of
So many things you would not let me speak of
Take pity on me)

Although "La Jolie Rousse" could conceivably have been inspired by Savinio's opera, there are quite a few differences between the two works as well. One suspects that their structural and lexical similarities can be explained by the fact that they derive from a common source: the liturgy of the Catholic Church. The last line, for example, which is identical in both poems, is the title of one of the Penitential Psalms and occurs in several other psalms in addition. Furthermore Psalm 51 in the Bible (50 in the Vulgate edition), which numerous composers have celebrated in music, bears the title "Miserere mei, Deus" ("Take Pity on Me, God"). One of the best known psalms, it plays a prominent role in the Catholic liturgy in particular. The Church's influence on "La Jolie Rousse" is also evident in the first three verses cited above, in which the poet asks for mercy three separate times and which form a moving prayer. Not only does their structure recall the Litanies of the Saints but the number three evokes numerological patterns associated with the Holy Trinity. To these examples should be added two other possible sources for Apollinaire's final line, two verses that he must have known by heart. One belongs to François Villon's famous "Epistre à ses amis" ("Letter to His Friends"), which begins with the exclamation: "Aiez pitié, aiez pitié de moy." The other was mentioned by Apollinaire himself in a letter to Louise Coligny de Châtillon dated 28 January 1915: "Une chanson d'amour qu'on chante ici finit 'Aie pitié de ton pauvre artilleur.' Toi tu en as pitié sans qu'on te le demande" ("A lovesong they sing here ends with the line 'Take pity on your poor artilleryman.' You have pity on him without even being asked").[13] Of course these lines were both inspired by the Catholic liturgy as well, especially Villon's verse in which he portrayed himself as a repentant sinner. In "La Jolie Rousse," therefore, whose Villonesque character is readily apparent, the poet's religious concerns and amorous preoccupations are reflected in the final line.

Francis Picabia

As soon as the war erupted Picabia found himself drafted into the French army, where he served as a general's chauffeur. Following a series of complex maneuvers, he arrived in America in June 1915 and made up his mind to stay there. In New York he encountered a number of his American friends, including de Zayas, Stieglitz, and Walter Conrad Arensberg, as well as several French acquaintances. No sooner did Picabia arrive in fact than he began to collaborate on the review *291*. Between June 1915 and February of the following year he contributed to virtually every issue. In addition to an article on modern art he published a series of mechanomorphic drawings that, as Michel Sanouillet remarks, "très souvent tournent au 'canular' poétique et visuel" ("very often involve practical jokes, both poetic and visual").[14] A Dada invention *par excellence*, whose influence would become widespread, Picabia's mechanomorphic style made its very first appearance in New York City. There, as a member of the editorial team, Picabia produced a group of object-portraits that led to the creation of an abstract mechanomorphic style which he would exploit until 1923 or so. Although the sources of Picabia's aesthetics have long been shrouded in mystery, recent research has shown that he was inspired by the abstract caricatures of his friend Marius de Zayas.[15]

Picabia published very few writings before 1917, when he suddenly became interested in poetry. Thereafter, however, he authored no fewer than eight volumes between 1917 and 1920. His greatest project was undoubtedly *391*, which saw the light of day on 25 January 1917. Destined to appear until 1924, the journal appeared in Barcelona, New York, Zurich, and Paris as the peripatetic Picabia sought a sympathetic milieu in which to develop his aesthetics. In April 1917 he returned to New York, where he collaborated on several avant-garde reviews edited by Marcel Duchamp and Henri-Pierre Roché. During this sojourn he probably presented Walter Conrad Arensberg with the manuscripts of *A quelle heure un train partira-t-il pour Paris?* and "Coeur couronne et miroir" that are now in the Francis Bacon Library.[16] One discovers with considerable astonishment that the latter institution is devoted to the English Renaissance. Established by Arensberg when he moved to California, it consists almost entirely of books and manuscripts from the sixteenth and seventeenth centuries. Formerly an important patron of the arts in New York, Arensberg became, as Kenneth Rexroth notes,

> the leading exponent of the Baconian heresy—the idea that Bacon wrote Shakespeare—to prove which he spent thousands. He was a close friend of Marcel Duchamp, and, aided by Duchamp, he built one of the two or three largest collections of modern painting in the world—now in the Philadelphia Museum. (It contains almost the entire *oeuvre* of Duchamp himself.)[17]

Before moving to California and founding his library, Arensberg played an important role in the New York avant-garde between 1911 and 1921. In addition, as the *Bulletin Dada* (5 February 1920) testifies, he was one of the "presidents" of the international Dada movement.

For Picabia *A quelle heure* seems to have constituted a sort of *poème-événément*, a work whose mysterious attraction could not be explained logically. In particular he must have been greatly impressed by the faceless man, for, like Apollinaire, he was to identify with this character in succeeding years. Curiously, Picabia devoted his art—like his life—to instability, to the continual search for impermanence. His aesthetics were built around the principle of perpetual novelty and were expressed by slogans such as "Fiche le camp est mon soutien" ("Moving on is what keeps me going") and "Toute conviction est une maladie" ("Every conviction is a disease") *(Unique Eunuque)*. And yet one finds certain themes, certain preoccupations, that spread across much of his poetry and painting. In the prose poem "Idéal doré par l'or" ("Ideal Gilded by Gold"), for instance, which was published in *391* in June 1917, one encounters an apparent reference to *A quelle heure*. What makes this example particularly important is that it occurs in a phrase often quoted by critics as the quintessence of Picabia's philosophy:

> Il faut traverser la vie, rouge ou bleu, tout nu, avec une musique de pêcheur subtil, prêt à l'extrême pour la fête.
>
> (Either red or blue, one should go through life stark naked accompanied by the music of a subtle fisherman, ready at every moment to celebrate.)[18]

This is not a description of Apollinaire's faceless musician so much as a synthesis of this character and the red, blue, and nude women who follow him in the pantomime. Just as Apollinaire's hero traverses the city and for that matter the stage, Picabia's personage makes his way through life. And how better describe the hypnotic power of the musician of Saint-Merry's tune than as "une musique de pêcheur subtil"? In both instances the character represents a fisherman of souls who is preparing (or prepared) for a carnal feast.[19] Picabia appears to have been captivated especially by the pantomime's freedom and by its erotic dimension.

In April 1918 Picabia also published a poem entitled "Poison ou revolver" in *Poèmes et dessins de la fille née sans mère*. Lacking any punctuation and written in a hermetic style, this work as well contains traces of *A quelle heure*. The words and phrases that seem to refer to Apollinaire's pantomime appear in italics below:

> Mante religieuse des images intérieures
> espèce de marotte qui gonfle la pudeur
> tous nous avons un petit livre de sournoiserie
> *suivant le mécanisme en idole*
>
> Mon clavier de *vieille femme infatuée*
> avec une tristesse infinie fait la grimace
> traduisant le désir de la roue fébrile
> du *drama* inscrit dans ma tête
>
> *Musiciens en silhouettes masquées*
> goinfres frénétiques des styles fondus
> sur la plage imprimée des champignons
> nous avançons dans la vie géniale
>
> Comme *les saccades du somnambulisme*
> trop tard dans ma vie d'alchimiste
> car l'image de soi gravite
> dans *le suicide*
>
> (Praying mantis of internal images
> sort of fad that inflates modesty

> we all have a little book of slyness
> *following the mechanism like an idol*
>
> My *old woman's infatuated* keyboard
> with infinite sadness makes a grimace
> translating the desire of the feverish wheel
> of the *drama* inscribed in my head
>
> *Musicians in masked silhouettes*
> frenetic guzzlers of dissolved styles
> on the beach imprinted with mushrooms
> we advance in genial life.
>
> Like *sleep-walking's fits and starts*
> too late in my alchemist life
> for one's self-image gravitates
> in *suicide*)[20]

If Picabia's intentions remain highly ambiguous, one detects a progression of key words, images, and ideas that seem to follow the pantomime's plot. To this progression should be added the "revolver" of the title as well. It is interesting to observe that according to Larousse one of the meanings of "marotte" (v. 2) is "tête de femme en bois ou en carton dont se servent les modistes" ("a woman's head made of cardboard or wood found in milliner's shops"). This is probably another reference to *A quelle heure*, therefore, which supports the hypothesis that Picabia chose the pantomime's outline for the skeleton of his poem. In both cases the erotic element is also quite pronounced.

It remains to mention two more references by Picabia to *A quelle un train partira-t-il pour Paris?* The first occurs in his *Jésus-Christ rastaquouère* (1920), in the section entitled "Amour d'intellectuels," which contains numerous obscene jokes. In particular one encounters a paragraph devoted to the "pénis aveugle" ("the blind penis") that ends with an amusing (and cynical) aphorism: "Notre phallus devrait avoir des yeux, grâce à eux nous pourrions croire un instant que nous avons vu l'amour de près" ("Our phallus should be provided with eyes, which would allow us to believe momentarily that we had glimpsed love at close range").[21] One suspects that this remark represents a conscious or an unconscious allusion to Apollinaire's phallic protagonist, who among other things has no eyes.

The last reference to the 1914 collaboration occurs in the poem

"Tambourin," which dates from 1924 and which contains the following lines:

> Les mouches voltigent avant de mourir
> Comme des petits projectiles
> La musique passe dans la rue
> Notre oreille la suit
> Il faut aller jusqu'au bout du monde . . .
>
> (The flies flit about before dying
> Like tiny projectiles
> Our ears follow the music
> As it passes by in the street
> One should go to the ends of the earth . . .)[22]

This time the pantomime is summarized in only five verses, reduced to an evocation of its beginning (the flies flitting around the luminous column) and its conclusion (death), with a momentary glimpse of the musician of Saint-Merry in the middle. The "musique qui passe dans la rue" alludes to the faceless man and his women who follow the bewitching melody. And the last two lines suggest the final verse of "Le Musicien de Saint-Merry" where the poet hears the sound of a flute dying away in the distance. As with "Idéal doré par l'or," the poem contains a verse that critics have often used to illustrate Picabia's philosophy: "Il faut aller jusqu'au bout du monde."

Guillaume Apollinaire

As noted previously, Apollinaire joined the French army when the war broke out and was assigned to the Artillery. Soon after volunteering he resumed his column in the *Mercure de France* and managed to publish a collection of poetry, *Case d'armons*. In addition he kept up a correspondence "à tuer les postes" ("which threatened to bury the post office"), of which he was proud, and remained in contact with most of his friends. On 4 April 1915, Apollinaire was sent to the front with an artillery unit. On 21 April he wrote to Lou with some interesting news about an invitation he had received: "On m'a écrit pour faire une exposition de mes poèmes-idéogrammes à New York. Si ça se fait, ce sera épatant" ("I have been invited to exhibit some of my ideographic poems in New York. If this works out, it will be marvelous").[23] The invitation had been extended by Marius de Zayas, who had been interested in the calligrams from the beginning and who had just published "Voyage" in *291*. It was accompanied by a copy of the first issue, which Apollinaire was to receive regularly until it ceased publication in 1916. For unknown reasons de Zayas's project was never carried out, although it would not have been difficult to arrange. One suspects that some of the poems in *Case d'armons* were originally written for this exhibition. It is even possible that this slim collection owed its typographical innovations to de Zayas's offer. Conceived in May and published soon thereafter (17 June 1915), it consisted of twenty-one poems written between the beginning of April and the middle of June—while Apollinaire was planning to exhibit his calligrams in New York.

On 20 November 1915, Apollinaire was transferred to the Infantry and promoted to second lieutenant. He was wounded on 17 March 1916 and was unable to resume his literary activities until August. By 1917, however, he had recovered from his wound and was involved in several theatrical projects. In addition to *Les Mamelles de Tirésias (The Breasts of Tiresias)*, which was performed in June, he was planning to transform *A quelle heure* into a ballet. Entitled *L'Homme sans yeux sans nez et sans oreilles (The Man With No Eyes No Nose and No Ears)*, this little-known work was never actually produced.[24] Apart from a few technical modifications the ballet followed the pantomime fairly closely. The principal differences between the two works were the following: (1) The original title was abandoned in favor of a shorter, more coherent title. (2) The original idea of a pantomime was replaced by the concept of a ballet. (3) The six scenes of *A quelle heure* were reduced to three tableaux. Apollinaire simplified the plot by eliminating the first scene and the second half of scene 4 (the historic processions). Similarly, he combined scene 3 with the first half of scene 4 (life and its variety) to form a single tableau. (4) The faceless man did not reappear at the end of the ballet. (5) the automatic king (Napoleon III) was never identified in the scenario. (6) Finally, Apollinaire modified the last scene so that it ended not with a suicide but with a general assassination. At the end a shot rings out, and the king and his single attendant collapse like puppets. Except for the conclusion, which retained its absurd character, the ballet version was more coherent and more conservative.

The fact that a composer named Soler Casabon wrote the music for *L'Homme sans yeux* allows us to date the ballet fairly precisely. In the spring of 1917 all the original collaborators, except Apollinaire, were far from Paris. Picabia had settled in New York for awhile, de Zayas was preoccupied with the Modern Gallery in the same city, and Savinio was about to leave for Macedonia (from Ferrara). The latter's absence was especially troubling to Apollinaire, as a letter he wrote to Léon Bakst on 10 April 1917, makes clear:

> Je ne connais malheureusement pas de musicien duquel je sois certain.
> Je viens d'achever une pièce et j'ai des sujets de ballet mais tout est subordonné en ce moment à la question du musicien.
>
> (Unfortunately I don't know any musicians I can count on.
> I have just finished a play and I have plans for several ballets but at present everything depends on finding a musician.)[25]

He was referring, naturally, to *Les Mamelles de Tirésias* and to *A quelle heure un train partira-t-il pour Paris?* It is known, for example, that both Georges Auric and Erik Satie had refused to write the music for *Les Mamelles de Tirésias*. Two months later, on 16 June 1917, an artistic soirée was sponsored by the Oeuvre du Soldat dans la Tranchée during which Apollinaire presented a lecture. His address was followed by a musical recital that included works by a number of different composers, including Soler Casabon, and that seems to have greatly interested the audience.[26] An anonymous review published in *Nord-Sud* in June included these remarks:

> Parmi les nouveaux musiciens qui nous furent révélés ces dernières semaines, citons tout particulièrement M. Soler Casabon.
> Son *Soliloque* pour piano, donné après la conférence d'Apollinaire, témoigne des dons remarquables. De l'audace, de la fraîcheur malgré la science indéniable, voilà ce qui nous fait espérer beaucoup de ce musicien qui vient de naître.
>
> (Among the new musicians who were revealed to us these past few weeks, M. Soler Casabon stands out.
> His *Soliloquy* for piano, which was performed following Apollinaire's lecture, reveals that he possesses remarkable gifts. The audacity of his music, its freshness despite its undeniable technical accomplishment, indicate that we can expect a brilliant future from this brand new musician.)

As this passage makes clear, Soler Casabon was unknown to the general public before this recital. Indeed Apollinaire probably encountered him for the first time at this very concert—too late to ask him to compose music for *Les Mamelles de Tirésias*, which was performed eight days later. Apollinaire seems to have been attracted to Casabon as much by his music, which had the same bold qualities as Savinio's compositions, as by the need to engage a composer.

Not surprisingly, perhaps, *Les Mamelles de Tirésias* itself contains numerous traces of *Les Chants de la mi-mort* and of *A quelle heure un train partira-t-il pour Paris?* Some of these traces, which constitute dramatic remembrances of the 1914 avant-garde, are not especially apparent, but others are easier to identify. In the first category, the revolver belonging to the People of Zanzibar (a single character representing a multitude in the tradition of *Ubu roi*) almost certainly derives from the pantomime. The same is undoubtedly true of the placards favored by Apollinaire, which are also to be found in *Ubu roi*. Like the pantomime's long-winded title, however, these objects have their source in the music hall where a series of placards were used to express various messages—which explains Savinio's reference to "le tradizioni del cartellone a successo" ("the traditional use of placards in a series") (see chapter 3). Finally, an identical pattern is discernible in Apollinaire's use of megaphones to amplify his characters' voices, a device much in evidence in *Les Mamelles de Tirésias*, which features a megaphone in the shape of a dice-box. The prologue implies that this was a souvenir of Apollinaire's service in the Artillery (cf. the poem "Du coton dans les oreilles"). Observing that the enemy guns have extinguished the stars, God employs a megaphone to command the French artillery to relight them once again.[27] It is evident nevertheless that this stage device was borrowed from the pantomime and from *Les Chants de la mi-mort*, where its function was identical. As with the placards and several characters, the megaphone's original source was the music hall and the circus—considered by the Futurists to represent the epitome of modern theater.

It is significant that Apollinaire had previously called attention to precisely this aspect of Futurist theater. Describing Marinetti's *Teatro di Varietà* (see chapter 3), he noted that it called for the following program:

> Incoraggiare in ogni modo il *genere* dei clowns e degli eccentrici americani, i loro effetti di grottesco esaltante, di dinamismo spaventevole, le loro grossolane trovate, le loro enormi brutalità, i loro panciotti a sorprese e i loro pantaloni profondi come stive di bastimenti, da cui uscirà con mille altre cose la grande ilarità futurista che deve ringiovanire la faccia del mondo.

(Encourage the performers to adopt the style of American clowns and slapstick artists, their exciting grotesqueness, their frightful dynamism, their crude tricks, their enormous brutality, their trick vests, and their trousers as deep as a ship's hold, from which will come (with a thousand other things) the great Futurist hilarity that is destined to rejuvenate the world).

Apollinaire's debt to this manifesto—already glaringly evident—is illustrated once again by his remarks during an interview three years later (published in *SIC* in August 1916). Speaking of the latest artistic tendencies, at a time when he himself was considering reviving *A Quelle heure* and was working on *Les Mamelles de Tirésias*, Apollinaire predicted the birth of a "théâtre de cirque . . . plus violent ou plus burlesque, plus simple aussi" ("circus theater . . . more violent or more ludicrous, more simple too") than before. Ironically these revolutionary remarks, which seemed to herald the appearance of a brand new aesthetics, went back to 1914 and to 1913. The "belle épopée où se rejoindraient tous les arts" ("beautiful epic which would incorporate all the arts") had already been created two years earlier by Apollinaire himself. Its author had already sensed its immense possibilities, had already intended to "s'exprimer au moyen du cinéma" ("express himself by means of the cinema"). Indeed this is one of the pantomime's most fascinating aspects. The staging of *A quelle heure* would have resulted in a work of art of the first order occupying a prominent place in the history of the cinema.

If *Les Mamelles de Tirésias* borrowed several props from the pantomime and from Savinio's opera, the more readily identifiable examples concern specific costumes. For example, one of the most important characters is modeled on the Yellow Man in *Les Chants de la mi-mort* and on the blue and red women in *A quelle heure*. As unlikely as it may seem at first, this person is none other than the neophyte feminist Thérèse, who deserts her husband and becomes Tiresias. This identification is unmistakable, for she is described in detail at the beginning of the play. There Apollinaire informs his readers that, in addition to wearing a long blue dress adorned with monkeys and painted fruits, she possesses a face to match—namely a "visage bleu." Another bizarre character, who has perhaps no direct antecedent but who obviously belongs to the same tradition, is the Fortune Teller whose skull is lighted electrically. There is an excellent chance that she is related, at least conceptually, to the protagonist of *A quelle heure*. For one recalls that, according to Savinio, the collaborators were thinking of representing their hero by a cluster of light bulbs. It remains to call attention to the newspaper kiosque in *Les Mamelles de Tirésias*, which was also inspired by the pantomime. According to several indications in the manuscript of *A quelle heure*, the Arc de Triomphe, Notre-Dame Cathedral, the Eiffel Tower, and the Tall Factory Chimney were supposed to be ambulatory monuments. Among other things, this explains why their names figure in the list of *dramatis personae*. Like its monumental antecedents the kiosque is both an animated and an ambulatory object. Not only is it able to move all over the stage, but it is listed with the other characters at the beginning of the play.

To this impressive list of references and influences should be added the most interesting character of all, whom I have kept for the end. This is the Parisian Journalist (who actually seems to be an American Journalist) who interviews Thérèse's husband after the husband has given birth to 40,049 children during the intermission. The reversal of sex roles has endowed him with incredible and instantaneous fecundity, though he comically attributes his new-found ability to "will power." According to Apollinaire's stage directions (act 2, scene 2) the Parisian Journalist makes his entrance dancing. While there are few indications as to the costume he is supposed to wear, one sentence catches the eye: "Sa figure est nue, il n'a que la bouche" ("His face is blank; he has only a mouth"). The feeling of *déjà vu* at this point is quite strong. This character is clearly a reincarnation of the faceless protagonist of *A quelle heure*, which Apollinaire was planning to revive as a ballet. In both cases the author apparently decided to restore his mouth. Since the journalist's main function is to serve as a foil for the husband, while parodying the screen image of the typical American, the costume's significance is difficult to grasp. In view of the faceless man's phallic origins, the portrait could conceivably be derogatory. On the other hand, since Apollinaire originally identified with this character, the reverse may be true as well.

An interesting epilogue is furnished by Giorgio de Chirico who, writing to a friend in 1948, deliberately exaggerated his brother's role in the genesis of *Les Mamelles de Tirésias*:

> In quanto alle *Mammelle* del buon Apollinaire, sono una farsa messa su da Savinio, quando Savinio era ancora a Parigi, e scriveva cose meno belle di quelle che fa ora. Il signor Apollinaire ha rifatto un po' l'ordito saviniano, guastandoci naturalmente ciò che ci poteva essere di buono, e poi lancia il libro come una pura *creazione*.

(As for the good Apollinaire's *Les Mamelles*, this farce was devised by Savinio when he was still in Paris and was writing less impressive things than he is now. Mister Apollinaire has changed things around a little, ruining everything with any potential of course, and now he is trying to pass it off as an original creation.)[28]

De Chirico was referring of course to *Les Chants de la mi-mort* which, as has been shown, have much in common with *Les Mamelles de Tirésias*. Besides the dramatic echoes already mentioned, Apollinaire's debt to Savinio's musical theories should also be noted. "Mariant souvent sans lien apparent comme dans la vie / Les sons les gestes les couleurs les cris les bruits" ("Combining sounds, gestures, colors, cries, and noises, often with no apparent connection as occurs in life"), as he says in the prologue, *Les Mamelles* adopted much of Savinio's 1914 aesthetics. The dissociation of musical and dramatic elements, the discontinuity produced by the People of Zanzibar's random noises—both of these ideas were borrowed by Apollinaire from his friend. In both works the music and the background noises—a sort of cubist punctuation—serve to underline the characters' actions. But if Savinio's influence on Apollinaire seems certain, there is no point in exaggerating its importance. Although Apollinaire borrowed several ideas from him, he refashioned them according to his own ends in a process well known to scholars. After all, a great artist is one who molds into a unique whole, according to his own inspiration, materials that he finds wherever he can. Apollinaire gives an excellent description of this process in *Les Peintres cubistes* when he compares the creative spirit to the chemistry of fire. "La flamme," he declares, "a la pureté qui ne souffre rien d'étranger et transforme cruellement en elle-même ce qu'elle atteint" ("A flame's purity suffers nothing extrinsic; whatever it touches is cruelly transformed into itself").[29]

7
Conclusion

To complete this history of the influence exerted by Apollinaire's faceless flute-player, one should mention the enormous popularity that de Chirico's mannequins enjoyed in their own right. Beginning with the Futurist Carlo Carrà, with whom he founded the *scuola metafisica* in 1917, de Chirico influenced a wide assortment of painters, including virtually all the Surrealists. Moreover, the mannequins were the most widely imitated elements of his iconography. To the mannequins in Carrà's works—all of which stem from de Chirico—should be added those in the paintings of Giorgio Morandi, one of the best modern Italian painters, and of Mario Sironi. The Germanic artists influenced by his mannequins include Max Ernst, George Grosz, and Oskar Schlemmer. Similar influence is evident in the works of Salvador Dali, Yves Tanguy, René Magritte, and Paul Delvaux. This list of painters, which could easily be expanded, confirms the power of Apollinaire's original inspiration and of de Chirico's subsequent metaphysical adaptations. Like his compatriot Magritte, Paul Delvaux was tremendously indebted to de Chirico, and there exists a curious painting of his entitled *Les Phases de la lune (Phases of the Moon)* (fig. 24). While this particular work exhibits no mannequin influence, it portrays a scene reminiscent of "Le Musicien de Saint-Merry." In the background a male flute-player (naked from the waist up and anatomically normal) is leading a procession of nude women. in the foreground a nude woman brazenly exposes herself to the view of two men, as if for sale (cf. also his *L'Eveil de la forêt*, 1939, on a similar theme). Is this perhaps another surprising example of Apollinarian inspiration? With the example of de Chirico still fresh in one's mind, one hesitates to dismiss this possibility completely.

While the mannequin figure can be seen to have roots reaching back as far as classical antiquity, only in the twentieth century has it been developed as a legitimate theme in itself. Historical analogues may be found in "sources" as disparate as Pygmalion's

24. Paul Delvaux, *Phases of the Moon*, 1939. Oil on canvas, 55" × 63". Collection The Museum of Modern Art, New York. Purchase.

statue, Don Juan's Commander, and Dr. Frankenstein's monster. Still, these are not really mannequins, nor do they play the role of the protagonist in their respective works. On the contrary, the mannequin seems to have been intended especially for our own industrialized, dehumanized age, whose strengths and weaknesses it symbolizes so well. Given the figure's sexless anonymity and its obvious association with machines—those beings Picabia termed "filles nées sans mère" (daughters born of no mother")—it is not surprising that it is often characterized as embodying evil forces, particularly in film and in science fiction. In this context the mannequin is remarkable for its pitiless stare, for its total lack of emotion. It appears to be the absence of compassion, more than anything else, that makes this character so threatening to the modern sensibility—itself partly shaped by the numerous cold-blooded social and political crimes of our century.

Conclusion

How strange, then, that at the beginning of the motif's tradition Apollinaire, Savinio, and de Chirico sympathized, and in fact *identified*, with the mannequin. As a symbol of the Poet, and of the creative artist in general, this character was very much the hero of their respective works. How are we to explain their basically positive attitude toward mannequins in the light of the opposite reaction by subsequent generations, a reaction that is seemingly much more justified? Perhaps the best solution is to view this contradiction (or evolution) in mannequin characterizations from a socio-historical perspective. Seen as the last brilliant flickerings of the optimistic spirit of the Belle Epoque, for example, the original three mannequins emerge as basically pre-World War I phenomena. Originating in 1913 and 1914, they belong to a prosperous era noteworthy for its stability, self-confidence, and enthusiasm, and it is not surprising that they should reflect these same qualities. It is quite possible, in addition, that these particular mannequins were conceived as yet another manifestation of *modernolatrie*, the enthusiasm for all things modern, which peaked in France at about that time. Be that as it may, one wonders what caused the initial mannequin personality to become corrupted at a later date. What happened to the figure's positive associations, so abundantly documented by the present study? The answer would seem to be that the change in artistic attitude toward mannequins—and hence in their characterization—corresponded to a general pessimistic shift in the collective modern psyche dating from the First World War. Already evident in the violent reactions of the Dada movement and prompted by the events of the war, the spread of postwar pessimism rendered the original mannequins obsolete. As a new generation of artists and writers came into being, they appropriated the still-powerful motif for their own ends. Thus, although the mannequin had originated as a symbol of individual creativity, it came to symbolize the sterile anonymity of modern existence.

Given the presence of other potential sources, it is risky to conclude from what we have seen that all modern mannequins stem from "Le Musicien de Saint-Merry." In fact, such is almost certainly not the case. One thinks in particular of the impetus given the motif in 1920 by Karel Čapek's play *R. U. R.*, which introduced the world to the character and term "robot."[1] The name itself (from the Czech word for worker) suggests that Čapek created this character by analogy with the specialized worker populations in ant and bee colonies. What is certain in any case is that he could also have drawn upon a very old tradition of automata in German literature (for example E. T. A. Hoffmann), a tradition that was surfacing at the time in films such as *Der Golem* (1916) and *Das Cabinet des Dr. Caligari* (1919). An analogous tradition existed in France as well. The automatic seductress in Villiers de l'Isle Adam's *Eve future* (1886), for example, reappeared in 1930 in Fritz Lang's well-known film *Metropolis*. Picabia's own situation epitomizes the confusion that exists with respect to multiple sources. In 1928 he wrote a scenario for the cinema, entitled *La Loi d'accomodation chez les borgnes (The Law of Accommodation for One-Eyed People)*, whose characters included several headless bodies and forty mannequins that engaged in automatic movements. But by this date Picabia had encountered so many influences that it is impossible to know where he found these particular characters. Despite the existence of several independent efforts along similar lines, Apollinaire's contribution to the mannequin tradition was clearly major. In the last analysis most, if not all, of the *faceless* mannequins in modern literature and art appear to descend from the musician of Saint-Merry.

Notes

Chapter 1. Introduction

1. See for example the cover of *Arts Magazine*, vol. 55, no. 10 (June 1981) and the article by Philip Smith, "Jedd Garet and the Atomic Age," pp. 158–60.

Chapter 2. Apollinaire's Mysterious Musician

1. The most important articles are the following: Philippe Renaud, " 'Ondes,' ou les métamorphoses de la musique," *Apollinaire et la musique,* ed. Michel Décaudin (Stavelot, Belgium: Les Amis de G. Apollinaire, 1967), pp. 21–32. This is expanded somewhat in his *Lecture d'Apollinaire* (Lausanne: L'Âge d'Homme, 1969), pp. 280–85. Also Octavio Paz, "El músico de Saint-Merry," *Traducción: literatura y literalidad* (Barcelona: Tusquets, 1971, pp. 52–66—originally printed in *Puertas al campo* (1966) and translated into English by Margaret Peden as " 'The Musician of Saint-Merry' by Apollinaire: A Translation and a Study," *L'Esprit Créateur,* vol. 10, no.4 (Winter 1970): 269–84. In addition the *Cahiers de l'Association Internationale des Etudes Françaises* [CAIEF], no.23 (May 1971), contain three important contributions by Philippe Renaud, S. I. Lockerbie, and Marc Poupon under the general heading "Le Musicien de Saint-Merry," pp. 177–220. Recently Madeleine Boisson has proposed yet another interpretation in *Apollinaire et les mythologies antiques* (Fasano: Schena and Paris: Nizet, 1989), pp. 334 ff. All translations from these and other works cited in the present study are my own.
2. Antoine Fongaro, " 'Le vingt et un du mois de mai . . .,' " *Revue des Lettres Modernes,* nos. 380–84 (1973), special issue *Guillaume Apollinaire 12,* p. 136.
3. For a more detailed analysis see Renaud, "Le Musicien de Saint-Merry," to which my discussion is partially indebted.
4. L. C. Breunig and J.-Cl. Chevalier, Introduction to *Méditations esthétiques: les peintres cubistes* by Guillaume Apollinaire (Paris: Hermann, 1965), p. 19.
5. S. I. Lockerbie also distinguishes between "Le thème du cortège" and "le thème de l'attroupement" ("the procession theme" and "the troupe theme") in "Le Musicien de Saint-Merry" and relates the three themes to the rest of Apollinaire's poetry.
6. Apollinaire used this image previously in "La Fiancée posthume" *(Le Poète assassiné),* a story published in *Le Matin* on 7 July 1911.
7. Renaud, "Le Musicien de Saint-Merry," p. 189.
8. See *Le Temps,* 25 November 1913, for an episode that involved an appeal to the Vatican. The Belgian Congo was in the news three more times during 1913 and 1914. In June 1913 Britain finally recognized the Belgian annexation of the Congo in 1908, and in the fall and winter of 1913 a sudden drop in the price of rubber threatened the economy. On 1 January 1914, the king announced a new colonial policy of administrative decentralization. *Le Temps* reported: "C'est à

Boma, et non plus à Bruxelles, que serait établi chaque année le projet de budget de la colonie. . . . A gauche on paraît craindre que le gouvernement catholique, qui est aux prises depuis deux ans avec de grosses difficultés suscitées par les missionnaires ne veuille chercher à profiter de la revision de la charte coloniale pour assurer de nouveaux avantages aux missions catholiques" ("The colonial budget would no longer be determined each year in Brussels but in Boma. . . . The leftists seem to fear that the Catholic government—which for two years has been grappling with huge problems created by the missionaries—will try to profit from the revision in the colonial charter in order to give the Catholic missions new powers") "La Réforme coloniale," 13 January 1914). If Apollinaire's reference was suggested by this news, as is probable, the poem may have been composed early in 1914.

9. Michel Décaudin following the three presentations in CAIEF, p. 366. Cf. Philippe Soupault's more sweeping statement that "tout l'effort d'Apollinaire, poète, tendait à créer de nouveaux mythes" ("Apollinaire's poetic efforts all tended to create new myths") in "Quand Apollinaire contait . . .," preface to Apollinaire's *Les Epingles* (Paris: Cahiers Libres, 1928), p. 20.

10. In *Eglise Saint-Merry de Paris, histoire de la paroisse et de la collégiale 700–1910*, 2 vols. (Paris: Oudin, 1911) the Abbé Baloche chronicles the repeated, unsuccessful attempts by the Saint-Merry clergy to get rid of the prostitutes surrounding their church.

11. Scott Bates, "taupe," *Petit Glossaire des mots libres d'Apollinaire* (Sewanee, Tenn.: privately printed, 1975), p. 99. See also "Pâquette," p. 70.

12. Pierre Caizergues, "Une précision," *Revue des Lettres Modernes*, nos. 276–79 (1971), special issue *Guillaume Apollinaire 10*, pp. 113–14. Guillaume Apollinaire," manuscrits et documents à la Bibliothèque nationale," *Que Vlo-Ve?*, 2d ser., no.12 (October-December 1984). pp. 8–11.

13. Victor Hugo immortalized the insurrection in *Les Misérables*, which includes a curious episode. After Inspector Javert, who has been spying on the revolutionaries, has been caught and tied to a post, Gavroche makes a request: " 'A propos, vous me donnerez son fusil!' Et il ajouta: 'Je vous laisse le musicien, mais je veux la clarinette' " (" 'Well now, give me his rifle!' And he added: 'I'll leave you the musician, but I want his clarinette' "). See *Les Misérables*, ed. Maurice Allem (Paris: Gallimard/Pléiade, 1964), p. 1137. Is this a simple coincidence? According to Fongaro, vv. 44–45 give us a glimpse of the class struggle, the "mockers" representing the capitalists who have exploited the misery of the proletariat. Thus Apollinaire seems to be referring to *Les Misérables* in particular.

14. See Jacques Hillairet, *Dictionnaire historique des rues de Paris* (Paris: Minuit, 1963), 2:465.

15. The epithet "maigre" ("meager") is puzzling applied to the powerful Suger. Is it possibly a misprint of "maître" ("master")?

16. Apollinaire, "Manuscrits et documents," pp. 10–11. See Hillairet, *Dictionnaire historique des rues de Paris*, 2:622.

17. This is probably the quarter Apollinaire took the Futurists to see in 1914. Giovanni Papini recounts that "la sera guidava ai *bals musette* o nelle straducole misteriose dove i negozianti di banane avevano i loro magazzini e i loro *bars*" ("at night he led us to the *bals musette* or through the mysterious lanes where the banana merchants had their stores and their *bars*"). See "Papini," *Omaggio ad Apollinaire*, ed. Giovanni Sangiorgi and Jacopo Recupero (Rome: Ente Premi Roma, 1960).

18. Renaud, in "Le Musicien de Saint-Merry," analyzes the different voices of the poem in detail.

19. "I sing the possibilities of myself" recalls a similar line from Whitman's *Song of Myself:* "I celebrate myself, and sing myself."

20. Mia *(Le poète assassiné,* "Colombe poignardée"), Pâquette ("La Chanson du Mal-Aimé"), Mavise *(Couleur du temps),* Ariane ("Arbre"), and Geneviève *(Histoire d'une famille vertueuse).*

21. Lockerbie, "Le Musicien de Saint-Merry," p. 204. Renaud believes that Apollinaire wishes to rid himself of a form of inspiration he had utilized widely in the past, based on suffering in love. Margaret Davies links the faceless man to his use of masks in other works as "les symboles d'une aliénation, qui nâit d'un sentiment d'amour trahi ou incomplet" ("symbols of an alienation stemming from a feeling of betrayal in love or unreciprocated love"). See her "Vitam Impendere Amori," *Revue des Lettres Modernes,* nos. 249–53 (1970), special issue *Guillaume Apollinaire 9,* pp. 81–82.

22. Scott Bates has arrived at the same conclusion by another route (as also the identification with the Dionysian procession). See his *Petit glossaire,* pp. 62–63.

23. Marc Poupon, in "Le Musicien de Saint-Merry" (p. 215), deduces that the protagonist is featureless because his head is that of a decomposing corpse, but there is nothing in the poem to support this view. In addition, he astutely observes that the bond between the women and their seducer is that of *fascination* but incorrectly links it to the *fascine* ("fagot," "bundle of sticks," hence "flute") instead of to the etymological *fascinum.* The latter term designated (1) a spell of witchcraft, (2) an amulet, often phallic, and (3) the phallus itself. See, for example, George Ryley Scott, *Phallic Worship* (London: T. Werner Laurie, 1941).

24. In *Le Poète assassiné* one encounters an old rabbi on this bridge but soon learns that Tristouse and her lover have come this way as well.

25. According to Fongaro in "Le Vingt et un du moi de mai . . .," (p. 136), the line evoking the Angelus comes from a popular song "L'Angélus de la mer": "Au loin, c'est l'Angélus, c'est l'Angélus qui sonne" ("In the distance, hear the Angelus, hear the Angelus ringing").

26. Baloche, *Eglise Saint-Merry de Paris,* 2:415–16 and 1:77 and 80 respectively. He describes the piper as "un petit joueur de cornemuse coiffé d'un bonnet tout pareil à celui que portent les jeunes Auvergnats" ("a little piper wearing a cap exactly like that worn by young men in Auvergne").

27. Hans Dobbertin has assembled some 154 historical texts (and illustrations) recounting the legend but omits Mérimée's version. See his *Quellensammlung zur Hamelner Rattenfängersage* (Göttingen: Schwartz, 1970). The Pied Piper also appears in "Poème lu au mariage d'André Salmon" (1909): "Il s'en allait au milieu des Hamlets blafards / Sur la flûte jouant les airs de la folie."

28. J. A. Dulaure, *Des divinités génératrices chez les anciens et les modernes* (Paris: Mercure de France, 1905), p. 240. See Gilbert Boudar et al., *La Bibliothèque de Guillaume Apollinaire,* vol. 1 (Paris: CNRS, 1983), p. 59.

29. Cf. the Brockhaus encyclopedia: "Richtig wird sein, dass sich eine alte Wandersage von einem Dämon" ("It is undoubtedly an ancient migratory myth about a demon").

30. S. Sophia Beale, *The Churches of Paris* (London: W. H. Allen, 1893), 252. André Breton and Gérard Legrand, writing in *L'Art magique* (Paris: Club Français du Livre, 1957), p. 172, describe the statue as a "Satan barbu et androgyne, devant qui deux anges balancent l'encensoir" ("a bearded androgynous satan before whom two angels swing a censer").

31. For Apollinaire's fly imagery see *L'Enchanter pourrissant,* ed. Jean Burgos (Paris: Lettres Modernes, 1972), pp. 164–67.

32. *Mordong,* proposed by Mario Richter, seems rather far-fetched

("Apollinaire e le 'mordonnantes mériennes,'" *Studi Francesi*, no. 49 [January–April 1973] p. 83). Cf. Paz, "El musico de Saint-Merry," p. 65.

33. Renaud, *Lecture d'Apollinaire*, p. 282.
34. Scott Bates, *Guillaume Apollinaire*, rev. ed. (Boston: Twayne, 1989), p. 121.
35. Friedrich Nietzsche, *Jenseits von Gut und Böse, Sämtliche Werke* (Stuttgart: Kröner, 1964), 3:230. The same passage appears in *Ecce Homo*, "Warum ich so gute Bücher schreibe," part 6, which is usually followed by the *Dionysos-Dithyramben*—including "Klage der Ariadne" ("Ariadne's Lament").
36. Cf. Martin P. Nilsson: "Der Phallos ist der stete Begleiter des Dionysos. Er scheint kaum in einer einzigendionysischen Prozession gefehlt zu haben" ("The phallus is the constant companion of Dionysos. It is scarcely lacking in a single Dionysian procession"). In "Der Phallos im Kult des Dionysos," *Geschichte der Griechischen Religion*, 2d ed. (Munich: C. H. Beck'sche, 1955), 1:590.
37. H. Jeanmaire, *Dionysos, histoire du culte de Bacchus* (Paris: Payot, 1951), p. 40.
38. Dulaure, *Des divinités génératrices chez les anciens et les modernes*, p. 98.
39. Among various indications of Apollinaire's familiarity with the Dionysian procession is his use of the word "canéphore" in several places. See for example his letter to Madeleine dated 19 September 1915 in *Tendre comme le souvenir* (Paris: Gallimard, 1952), p. 150.
40. Jeanmaire, *Dionysos, histoire du culte de Bacchus*, p. 39. Nilsson, *Geschichte der Griechischen Religion*, p. 593.
41. See Monique Jutrin, "La Présence du conteur dans la poésie d'Apollinaire," *Regards sur Apollinaire conteur*, ed. Michel Décaudin (Paris: Lettres Modernes, 1975), p. 10, and Bates, *Guillaume Apollinaire*, p. 130.
42. "Echos et on-dit des lettres et des arts," *L'Europe Nouvelle*, 24 August 1918. Reprinted in Apollinaire, *Oeuvres complètes*, ed. Michel Décaudin (Paris: Balland-Lecat, 1965–66), 2:750.
43. *Le Poète assassiné* (Paris: Gallimard, 1947), p. 37. Apollinaire's worldview is probably indebted to two illustrious predecessors: Dante and Empedocles. In the *Paradiso* the former depicts (divine) love as the power by which the universe is governed. In the latter's cosmology Love is the universal unifying principle and Hatred the divisive principle. See Lionel Follet, "Apollinaire lecteur d'Empédocle," *Revue des Lettres Modernes*, nos. 576–81 (1980), special issue *Guillaume Apollinaire 15*, p. 59–68.
44. André Breton, "Du surréalisme en ses oeuvres vives," *Manifestes du surréalisme* (Paris: Gallimard/Idées, 1965), p. 181.

Chapter 3. A Train Leaves for Paris

1. The Francis Bacon Library, Claremont, California. See Guillaume Apollinaire, *A quelle heure un train partira-t-il pour Paris?*, ed. Willard Bohn (Montpellier: Fata Morgana, 1982). A partial copy, as well as an earlier manuscript, belong to the Marius de Zayas Archives in Seville. For the later documents see Guillaume Apollinaire, *A quelle heure un train partira-t-il pour Paris?*, ed. Henrik van Scaldegem (Ghent: Arteveld, 1986).
2. The best study of his important role in the New York avant-garde is a posthumous article by de Zayas himself: "How, When, and Why Modern Art Came to New York," ed. Francis M. Naumann, *Arts Magazine*, vol. 54, no. 8 (April 1980): 96–126. See also Craig R. Bailey, "The Art of Marius de Zayas," *Arts Magazine*, vol. 53, no. 1 (September 1978): 136–44; Willard Bohn, "The Abstract

Vision of Marius de Zayas," *Art Bulletin*, vol. 62, no. 3 (September 1980): 434–52; and Douglas Hyland, *Marius de Zayas: Conjuror of Souls* (Lawrence, Kans.: Spencer Museum of Art, 1981).

3. My reconstruction of de Zayas's Paris visit is based on his correspondence with Stieglitz in the Alfred Stieglitz Archive, Collection of American Literature, Beinecke Rare Book and Manuscript Library, Yale University.

4. "En Amérique," *Paris-Journal*, 24 May 1914. Reprinted in Guillaume Apollinaire, *Petites Flâneries d'art*, ed. Pierre Caizergues (Montpellier: Fata Morgana, 1980), pp. 73–74.

5. "Marius de Zayas," *Paris-Journal*, 8 July 1914. Reprinted in Guillaume Apollinaire, *Chroniques d'art*, ed. L. C. Breunig (Paris: Gallimard, 1960), pp. 408–9.

6. The manuscripts for "Paysage" are reproduced in de Zayas, "How, When, and Why," p. 112. Those for "Lettre-Océan" appear in P. A. Jannini, *Le avanguardie letterarie nell'idea critica di Guillaume Apollinaire* (Rome: Bulzoni, 1971), pp. 207–8. Those for "Coeur couronne et miroir" belong to the Francis Bacon Library and are produced in Williard Bohn, *The Aesthetics of Visual Poetry, 1914–1928* (Cambridge: Cambridge University Press, 1986), pp. 63–65.

7. "Marius de Zayas," *Paris-Journal*, 19 July 1914.

8. Letter from Marie Rapp to Alfred Stieglitz dated 14 September 1914. Alfred Stieglitz Archive, Yale University.

9. See for example Massimo Carrà et al., *Metafisica* (Milan: Mazzotta, 1968); Ugo Piscopo, *Alberto Savinio* (Milan: Mursia, 1973); and Franco Russoli, ed. *Alberto Savinio* (Milan: Electa, 1976).

10. "Musique nouvelle," *Paris-Journal*, 24 May 1914. Reprinted in *Chroniques d'art*, p. 382.

11. "Albert Savinio," *Mercure de France*, 1 June 1914. Reprinted in Guillaume Apollinaire, *Anecdotiques*, ed. Marcel Adéma (Paris: Gallimard, 1955), p. 181.

12. "Dessin et musique," *Paris-Journal*, 7 July 1914. Reprinted in *Petites Flâneries d'art*, p. 126. For a more detailed discussion of the relations between Apollinaire and Savinio during this period, including the weekly dinners sponsored by *Paris-Journal*, see Willard Bohn, "Sur la Butte: Apollinaire and Savinio," *Que Vlo-Ve?*, Bulletin International des Etudes sur Apollinaire, 2d ser., no. 13 (January–March 1985), pp. 5–9.

13. On 11 April 1913, Stieglitz wrote to Arthur B. Carles: "Picabia left yesterday. All at '291' will miss him . . . Picabia came to '291' virtually daily and I know he will miss the little place quite as much as we miss him . . . Even Picabia was astonished at de Zayas' ability. . . ." Alfred Stieglitz Archive, Yale University.

14. J.-Cl. Chevalier and L. C. Breunig, "Apollinaire et *Les Peintres cubistes*," *Revue des Lettres Modernes*, nos. 104–7 (1964), special issue *Guillaume Apollinaire 3*, pp. 108 and 112 (n. 36).

15. John Weichsel, "Cosmism or Amorphism," *Camera Work*, nos. 24–43 (April–July 1913): 80.

16. Maurice Aisen, "The Latest Evolution in Art and Picabia," *Camera Work*, special issue June 1913, p. 18.

17. William Agee, "New York Dada, 1910–1930," *The Avant-Garde*, ed. Thomas B. Hess and John Ashberry (London: Collier-Macmillan, 1968), pp. 105–113. This volume corresponds to the *Art News Annual* for 1968.

18. "Le Salon des Indépendants," *L'Intransigeant*, 2 March 1914. Reprinted in *Chroniques d'art*, p. 349.

19. "Le 30ᵉ Salon des Indépendants," *Les Soirées de Paris*, no. 22 (March 1914), p. 188.

20. "Francis Picabia a envoyé à l'exposition d'Amsterdam toute une série d'aquarelles qu'il a peintes ce printemps dans le Midi. Il y a là, notamment, *Force comique, Horrible Douleur, Choix admirable à voir, En badinant, Les Sources des eaux,* etc." ("Francis Picabia has sent a whole series of watercolors to the Amsterdam show that he painted this spring in the South of France. These include *Comic Force, Horrible Pain, Admirable Choice to Behold, While Bantering, The Springs,* etc."). See "Aquarelles de Picabia," *Paris-Journal*, 29 May 1914.

21. "Francis Picabia a achevé récemment deux grands tableaux pour le Salon d'Automne, *Mariage comique* et *Je revois par le souvenir ma chère Udnie.* Il va se mettre à *Horrible Douleur* qui complétera son envoi" ("Francis Picabia has recently finished two large paintings for the Salon d'Automne, *Comic Marriage* and *I See My Dear Udnie Once Again in My Memory.* He is about to begin *Horrible Pain* which will complete the works he is sending"). See "Francis Picabia," *Paris-Journal*, 13 July 1914.

22. "Pour le Salon d'Automne," *Paris-Journal*, 25 July 1914. Reprinted in *Petites Flâneries d'art*, p. 148 (where it is inadvertently dated 23 July).

23. Guillaume Apollinaire, *Souvenirs de la Grande Guerre*, ed. Pierre Caizergues (Montpellier: Fata Morgana, 1980), p. 17.

24. De Zayas had put on a pantomime himself in New York in 1912, exemplifying what he referred to as a "theater of caricature."

25. Guillaume Apollinaire, *Oeuvres poétiques*, ed. Marcel Adéma and Michel Décaudin (Paris: Gallimard/Pléiade, 1965), p. 562.

26. Le Baron Mollet, "Soirées à Paris et Ballets russes avec Guillaume Apollinaire," *Les Lettres Françaises*, 11 November 1948, p. 3.

27. Alberto Savinio, "Il poeta assassinato," *La Voce*, vol. 8, nos. 11–12 (31 December 1916), p. 439.

28. See for example the photograph in Francis Lacassin, *Louis Feuillade* (Paris: Seghers, 1916), p. 186.

29. "Fantômas," *Mercure de France*, 16 July 1914. Reprinted in *Anecdotiques*, pp. 184–85.

30. Guillaume Apollinaire, *Tendre comme le souvenir* (Paris: Gallimard, 1952), p. 141.

31. For other examples of a phallic Eiffel Tower in Apollinaire's work see Scott Bates, *Petit Glossaire des mots libres d'Apollinaire* (Sewanee, Tenn.: privately printed, 1975), p. 102.

32. Jean Levaillant, "L'Espace dans *Calligrammes*," *Revue des Lettres Modernes*, nos. 217–22 (1969), special issue *Guillaume Apollinaire 8*, p. 51.

33. "Médaillon: Un Fauve," *Chroniques d'art*, p. 65.

34. André Breton and Gérard Legrand, *L'Art magique* (Paris: Club Français du Livre, 1957), p. 143.

35. Two recent books have considerably expanded our knowledge in this area: Jean-Claude Blachère, *Le Modèle nègre* (Dakar, Abidjan, and Lomé: Nouvelles Editions Africaines, 1981) and Katia Samaltanos, *Apollinaire: Catalyst for Primitivism, Picabia, and Duchamp* (Ann Arbor: UMI Research Press, 1984).

36. "Alexandre Archipenko," in *Siebzehnte Ausstellung: Alexandre Archipenko* (Berlin: Der Sturm, 1914). Reprinted in *Chroniques d'art*, p. 355.

37. Blaise Cendrars, *Oeuvres complètes* (Paris: Denoël, 1963), vol. 1, pp. 95–96.

38. John Beattie, *Other Cultures: Aims, Methods, and Achievements in Social Anthropology* (New York: Free Press, 1964), p. 206.

39. A similar idea is expressed in "Les Collines" ("The Hills"): "Profondeurs de la conscience / On vous explorera demain / Et qui sait quels êtres vivants / Seront

tirés de ces abîmes / Avec des univers entiers" ("Depths of consciousness / You will be explored tomorrow / And who knows what living beings / Will emerge from this abyss / With whole new universes").

40. Guillaume Apollinaire, L'Anti-tradition futuriste, Oeuvres complètes, ed. Michel Décaudin (Paris: Balland Lecat, 1965–66), 3:876a–c.

41. "Les dramaturges s'ils s'en tiennent aux formules réalistes du siècle dernier seront vite dépassés par le cinématographe, dont les ressources scéniques sont infiniment plus nombreuses que celles des théâtres les plus perfectionnés. Aussi le peuple ne s'y trompe et le cinématograph tend à remplacer le théâtre" ("If they retain the realistic formulas of the previous century, the playwrights will quickly be overshadowed by the cinema, whose technical resources are infinitely more numerous than those of the most accomplished theaters. Thus the masses are not mistaken, and the cinema is tending to replace the theater"). See Apollinaire, "La Loi de renaissance," La Démocratie sociale, 7 July 1912. Reprinted in Apollinaire et La Démocratie Sociale, ed. Pierre Caizergues (Paris: Lettres Modernes, 1969), p. 36.

42. P. A. Jannini, La fortuna di Apollinaire in Italia (Milan: Istituto Editoriale Cisalpino, 1965), 2d ed.

43. Marie-Jeanne Durry, Guillaume Apollinaire: "Alcools" (Paris: SEDES, 1956–64), 2:231.

44. In this connection it is significant that the origins and symptoms of Dada tended to be dramatic in nature. See, for example, Roger Shattuck, "The Aesthetics of Dada," Dada/Surrealism, no. 2 (1972): 7–10. For in its transition from life as performance to performance as life, Dada was inherently theatrical. While something analogous to this philosophy is to be found in Apollinaire's pantomime, its ties with Dada are likewise evident in its choice of technical means, i. e., in its theatrical language. Cf. Tristan Tzara's description of the soirées at the Cabaret Voltaire in Zurich: "Des personnages en édition unique apparaissent, récitent ou se suicident" ("characters of unique edition appear, recite, or commit suicide"). See "Chronique Zurichoise 1915–1919" in his Oeuvres complètes, (Paris: Flammarion, 1975), 1:561.

Chapter 4. Alberto Savinio at Home

1. Raymond Pouillart, "Apollinaire et quelques musiciens," Apollinaire et la musique, ed. Michel Décaudin (Paris: Minard, 1967), p. 59.

2. "L'Audition des oeuvres musicales de M. Albert Savinio," Les Soirées de Paris, No. 25 (15 June 1914). "Albert Savinio," Mercure de France, 1 June 1914; reprinted in Guillaume Apollinaire, Anecdotiques, ed. Marcel Adéma (Paris: Gallimard, 1955), p. 181.

3. "L'Audition des oeuvres musicales de M. Albert Savinio"—see the preceding note.

4. "Musique nouvelle," Paris-Journal, 24 May 1914. Reprinted in Guillaume Apollinaire, Chroniques d'art, ed. L. C. Breunig (Paris: Gallimard, 1955), p. 383.

5. In 1938 Les Chants de la mi-mort was published by H. Parisot in Paris. For a more recent edition see Alberto Savinio, Vita dei fantasmi (Milan: Scheiwiller, 1962) as well as Vie des fantômes, trans. André Pieyre de Mandiargues (Paris: Flammarion, 1965). The references between parentheses in the present text refer to the latter edition.

6. In 1915 Savinio published an extract of an unknown song, taken from Les

Chants de la mi-mort, which evokes the execution of General Ramorino: ". . . Tout était doux de lumière dans la citadelle de Turin—22 Maggio 1849—Le ciel de soie gris-perle. La bannière de l'Hôtel Lutetia claquait comme une langue qui savoure de la Bénédictine. Ah, mes amis, è terribile! è terribile! è terribile!" (". . . Everything was bathed in a soft light in the citadel at Turin—22 May 1849—The sky of pearl grey silk. The Hotel Lutetia's banner clacked in the wind like a tongue savoring Benedictine. Ah, my friends, it's terrible! it's terrible! it's terrible!"). See his "Dammi l'anatema, cosa lasciva," *291*, no. 4 (June 1915), p. 4.

7. For a discussion of *Les Chants de la mi-mort* in the context of Lautréamont and André Breton see Renzo Paris, "La volontà formativa nei 'Canti' di Alberto Savinio," *Quaderni del Novecento Francese*, no. 2 (1974): 181–88.

8. See the painting entitled *Natura morta: Torino a primavera* in *L'opera completa di Giorgio de Chirico, 1908–1924*, ed. Maurizio Fagiolo dell'Arco (Milan: Rizzoli, 1984), plate 15.

9. Antoine Fongaro, review of *Apollinaire et l'homme sans visage* by Willard Bohn in *Rivista di Letterature Moderne e Comparate*, 39 (1986): 346.

10. André Breton, *Anthologie de l'humour noir* (Paris: Pauvert, 1966), p. 368.

11. For a discussion of Nietzsche's influence on de Chirico's paintings see James Thrall Soby, *Giorgio de Chirico* (New York: Museum of Modern Art, 1955), pp. 27–28.

12. See for example Nietzsche's "Letter to a Professor," dated 6 January 1989, in which he wrote: "Je me suis réservé une petite chambre d'étudiant qui est située en face du Palais Carignan (dans lequel je suis né sous le nom de Victor Emmanuel)" ("I have taken a simple student's room across from the Carignan Palace, in which I was born under the name of Vittorio Emanuele"). Cited in Breton, *Anthologie de l'humour noir*, p. 172.

13. See *L'opera completa di Giorgio de Chirico*, p. 89, D 16, which is mistakenly titled "Portrait de Guillaume Apollinaire." In actuality the drawing has no title.

14. Ibid., p. 92, plate 66.

15. See Apollinaire's letters to Paul Guillaume dated 18 April, 6 May, and 16 May 1915. Guillaume Apollinaire, *Oeuvres complètes*, ed. Michel Décaudin (Paris: Balland-Lecat, 1965–66) 4:871–72.

16. See the letter from Giorgio de Chirico to Francesco Meriano, dated 20 July 1918, which is cited in P. A. Jannini, *La fortuna di Apollinaire in Italia* (Milan: Istituto Editoriale Cisalpino, 1965), 2d ed., p. 74. See also Giorgio de Chirico, *Memorie della mia vita* (Milan: Rizzoli, 1962), pp. 72–73. Savinio expressed a similar opinion toward the end of his article "In Poetae memoriam," *L'Esprit nouveau*, no. 26 (October 1924), unpaginated.

17. "Musique nouvelle," *Paris-Journal*, 24 May 1914; reprinted in *Chroniques d'art*, p. 384.

18. We also know that the statue in two of de Chirico's paintings, *The Enigma of a Day* (1914) and *The Serenity of the Scholar* (1914), represents Cavour, who is recognizable from his glasses. See Joseph C. Sloane, "Giorgio de Chirico and Italy," *Art Quarterly*, vol. 21, no.1 (Spring 1958): 9–10. However one wonders if this statue, whose hair can be seen clearly, is identical to that of 1913.

19. Savinio's "Dammi l'anatema, cosa lasciva" contains the following passage: "TRECENTO. Désormais l'artiste créateur est homme politique, redingoté, statufié: 'dice Mario Filelfo che l'altissimo Poeta sostenne in nome de' Fiorentini quattordici ambascerie' (*Storia de la letteratura italiana*, del cav. Giuseppe Maffei, cappellano audico di S. A. Massimiliano Duca di Baviera)" ("THE FOURTEENTH CENTURY. Henceforth the creative artist is a politician, dressed in a frock coat

and changed into a statue: 'Mario Filelfo says that the reverend Poet occupied fourteen diplomatic posts on behalf of the Florentines' [Storia de la letteratura italiana, by Giuseppe Maffei]").

20. Savinio, *Vie des fantômes*, p. 27.
21. Letter from Guillaume Apollinaire to Paul Guillaume dated 16 May 1915. See note 15.
22. Luigi Rognoni, "Savinio musicista," in *Alberto Savinio*, (Milan: Electa, 1976), p. 27.

Chapter 5. Giorgio di Chirico among the Mannequins

1. James Thrall Soby, *Giorgio de Chirico* (New York: Museum of Modern Art, 1955), p. 32. Unless otherwise noted the paintings cited in this chapter may be found in this volume and/or *L'opera completa di Giorgio de Chirico, 1908–1924*, ed. Maurizio Fagiolo dell'Arco (Milan: Rizzoli, 1984).
2. Isabella Far, *De Chirico*, trans. Joseph M. Bernstein (New York: Abrams, 1968), p. 14.
3. "Nouveaux Peintres," *Paris-Journal*, 14 July 1914. Reprinted in Guillaume Apollinaire, *Chroniques d'art*, ed. L. C. Breunig (Paris: Gallimard, 1955), p. 411.
4. "G. de Chirico—Pierre Brune," *L'Intransigeant*, 30 October 1913. For a study of Apollinaire's criticism of de Chirico, including the text cited above, see Willard Bohn, "Metaphysics and Meaning: Apollinaire's Criticism of Giorgio de Chirico," *Arts Magazine*, vol. 55 no. 7 (March 1981): 109–13.
5. "Echos et on-dit des Lettres et des Arts," *L'Europe Nouvelle*, 13 April 1918. Reprinted in *Chroniques d'art*, p. 432.
6. See Soby, *Giorgio de Chirico*, pp. 45 and 64.
7. Pierre-Marcel Adéma, *Guillaume Apollinaire* (Paris: Table Ronde, 1968), plate 32.
8. Raffaele Carrieri, *Iconografia italiana di Apollinaire* (Milan: Scheiwiller, 1954), frontispiece. This volume also contains a drawing by Savinio entitled "Apollinaire all'Ospedale Italiano di Parigi."
9. Soby, *Giorgio de Chirico*, pp. 44–45.
10. Pierre Cailler, ed., *Guillaume Apollinaire: Documents iconographiques* (Geneva: Cailler, 1965), plate 81.
11. Cf. Carlo Carrà's testimony: "Quando io vidi nella primavera del '14, nella casa di Apollinaire, un suo quadro rappresentante una torre grigia, solitaria, dietro alla quale si scorgevano linee sinuose di colline azzurrine, sentii subito di trovarmi di fronte ad una individualità artistica nuova" ("When, in Apollinaire's house in spring 1914, I saw one of [de Chirico's] paintings depicting a grey, solitary tower, behind which one glimpsed the sinuous lines of azure hills, I immediately understood that I was in the presence of a new artistic talent"). See his article entitled "Giorgio de Chirico," *L'Ambrosiano*, 6 May 1931; reprinted in Carlo Carrà, *Tutti gli scritti*, ed. Massimo Carrà (Milan: Feltrinelli, 1978), p. 513.
12. *Apollinaire*, ed. Jean Adhémar et al. (Paris: Bibliothèque nationale, 1969), no. 330.
13. André Breton, *Le Surréalisme et la peinture* (Paris: Gallimard, 1928), p. 38. Soby, *Giorgio de Chirico*, p. 46.
14. Soby, *Giorgio de Chirico*, p. 46.
15. Scott Bates, *Guillaume Apollinaire* (Boston: Twayne, 1967), p. 125.

16. Guillaume Apollinaire, *Tendre comme le souvenir* (Paris: Gallimard, 1952), p. 131.

17. André Breton, *Anthologie de l'humour noir* (Paris: Pauvert, 1966), p. 368. See also his "Lettre à Robert Amadou," *Revue métapsychique*, no. 27 (January–February 1954). Reprinted in André Breton, *Perspective cavalière*, ed. Marguerite Bonnet (Paris: Gallimard, 1970), pp. 38–45.

18. Giorgio de Chirico, *Hebdomeros* (Paris: Flammarion, 1964), pp. 133–34. It is Hebdomeros who is speaking.

19. Friedrich Nietzsche, *Jenseits von Gut and Böse, Sämtliche Werke*, (Stuttgart: Kröner, 1964) 7: 230. The same text appears in *Ecce Homo*, "Warum ich so gute Bücher schreibe," sect. 6.

20. Breton, *Le Surréalisme et la peinture*, pp. 35–36.

21. Derek Beales, *The Risorgimento and the Unification of Italy* (London: Allen and Unwin; New York: Barnes and Noble, 1971), p. 76.

22. See his remarks concerning the *daïmons* of Heraclitus of Ephesus in "Zeusi l'esploratore," *Valori Plastici*, 15 November 1918. Reprinted in Massimo Carrà, *Metafisica* (Milan: Mazzotta, 1968), pp. 202–3.

23. Alberto Savinio, "Dammi l'anatema, cosa lasciva," *291*, no. 4 (June 1915), p. 4.

24. De Chirico's symbolic system is explored more extensively in Willard Bohn, "Phantom Italy: The Return of Giorgio de Chirico," *Arts Magazine*, vol. 56, no. 2 (October 1981): 132–35 and "Giorgio de Chirico and the Paradigmatic Method," *Gazette des Beaux-Arts*, vol. 106, nos. 1398–99 (July–August 1985): 35–41. I attempt to apply the insights acquired in these two articles to de Chirico's entire metaphysical corpus in "Giorgio de Chirico and the Solitude of the Sign," forthcoming in the *Gazette des Beaux-Arts*.

25. Giorgio de Chirico, *Il meccanismo del pensiero: critica, polemica, autobiografia, 1911–1943*, ed. Maurizio Fagiolo (Turin: Einaudi, 1985), pp. 36–37.

26. Raffaele Carrieri, *Giorgio de Chirico* (Milan: Garzanti, 1962). Reprinted in his *Pittura e scultura d'avanguardia in Italia (1890–1955)* (Milan: Conchiglia, 1955).

27. Carrieri, *Pittura e scultura d'avanguardia in Italia*, pp. 127–28. He makes essentially the same claim in *Forme* (Milan: Milano-Sera, 1949) in the section "Giorgio de Chirico," pp. 71–87.

28. Soby, *Giorgio de Chirico*, p. 97.

29. Sergio Zoppi, *Al festino di Esopo* (Rome: Bulzoni, 1979), p. 110.

30. Adéma, *Guillaume Apollinaire*, p. 232.

31. André Breton and Philippe Soupault would evoke this painting seven years later in *Les Champs magnétiques*, in the next-to-last paragraph of "La Glace sans tain," which begins: "La fenêtre creusée dans notre chair s'ouvre sur notre coeur" ("The window hollowed out of our flesh opens onto our heart").

32. See for example Scott Bates, "huître," *Petit Glossaire des mots libres d'Apollinaire* (Sewanee, Tenn.: privately printed, 1975), p. 45.

33. For the voyage theme in de Chirico's works see Marianne W. Martin, "Reflections on De Chirico and *Arte Metafisica*," *The Art Bulletin*, vol. 60, no. 2 (June 1978): 346–47; 352–53.

34. Soby, *Giorgio de Chirico*, p. 98. André Breton and Gérard Legrand, *L'Art magique* (Paris: Club Français du Livre, 1957), p. 224.

35. At this stage the mask-scar, which had become a sort of enormous eye, signified that the mannequin was a phantom, that it incarnated a primordial force. See in this connection "Zeusi l'esploratore," in which de Chirico explains that the eye is the symbol of the Heraclitian *daïmon*.

Chapter 6. The Dawn of a New Age

1. Marius de Zayas, "Watch Their Steps," *291*, no. 3 (May 1915), p. 4.
2. For an analysis of this composition see Willard Bohn, *The Aesthetics of Visual Poetry, 1914–1928* (Cambridge: Cambridge University Press, 1986), pp. 185–203.
3. See ibid., pp. 9–24, for a detailed analysis of this work.
4. The Marius de Zayas Archives in Seville contain an unsigned contract between de Zayas and Savinio that was drafted in preparation for his American tour.
5. Michel Sanouillet, *Francis Picabia et "391"* (Paris: Losfeld, 1966), p. 37; also *Dada à Paris* (Paris: Pauvert, 1967), p. 237.
6. Alberto Savinio, *Vie des fantômes* (Paris: Flammarion, 1965), pp. 27–28.
7. This fact is reported by Giorgio de Chirico in *Memorie delle mia vita* (Milan: Rizzoli, 1962).
8. A poem entitled "La festa muratoria" bears the notation: "Ferrare, 22 mai 1917." First published in the *Antologia della Diana* (Naples, 1918), it is reprinted in Massimo Carrà et al., *Metafisica* (Milan: Mazzotta, 1968), p. 261.
9. See P. A. Jannini, *La fortuna di Apollinaire in Italia* (Milan: Istituto Editoriale Cisalpino, 1965), 2d ed., pp. 135–36.
10. Cited in ibid., p. 97, n.47.
11. Alberto Savinio, "Scambi," *La Rassegna d'Italia*, vol. 1, no. 5 (May 1946): 51–53.
12. Savinio, *Vie des fantômes*, pp. 25–26.
13. Guillaume Apollinaire, *Lettres à Lou*, ed. Michel Décaudin (Paris: Gallimard, 1969), p. 139.
14. Michel Sanouillet, *"391," revue publiée de 1917 à 1924 par Francis Picabia* (Paris: Terrain Vague, 1960), p. 10.
15. Willard Bohn, "The Abstract Vision of Marius de Zayas," *The Art Bulletin*, vol. 62, no. 3 (September 1980): 434–52, and "Picabia's 'Mechanical Expression' and the Demise of the Object," *The Art Bulletin*, vol. 67, no. 4 (December 1985): 673–77.
16. The Library possesses other documents that testify to Picabia's and Arensberg's friendship: (1) a copy of *Les Soirées de Paris*, nos. 26–27 (the issue that contains "Coeur couronne et miroir"); we know that Picabia was a subscriber—see Pierre-Marcel Adéma, *Guillaume Apollinaire* (Paris: Table Ronde, 1968), p. 232; (2) a copy of *Poèmes et dessins de la fille née sans mère* (1918) dedicated "à Walter Conrad Arensberg / Francis Picabia / 16 janvier 1918 / Lausanne"; (3) a copy of *Jésus-Christ rastaquouère* (1920) dedicated "à Walter Conrad Arensberg / Très amicalement / Francis Picabia / Si vous possédez / vous n'avez plus qu'à chier / F. P."; (4) a copy in very poor condition of Apollinaire's *Le Poète assassiné* dedicated "A Gabrielle et Francis / Picabia / leur ami / Guillaume Apollinaire," dated October 1916.
17. Kenneth Rexroth, *Assays* (New York: New Directions, 1961), p. 155.
18. Francis Picabia, *Ecrits, 1913–1920*, ed. Olivier Revault d'Allonnes (Paris: Belfond, 1975), p. 63.
19. Compare the passage in which Nietzsche describes Dionysos as "the born rat-catcher of consciences, whose voice can descend into the underworld of every soul" (see chapter 2).
20. Picabia, *Ecrits, 1913–1920*, p. 87.
21. Ibid., p. 244.

22. Francis Picabia, *Ecrits, 1921–1953 et posthumes,* ed. Olivier Revault d'Allonnes and Dominique Bouissou (Paris: Belfond, 1978), p. 135.

23. Apollinaire, *Lettres à Lou,* p. 308. See also pp. 314 and 431, which are concerned with *291.*

24. For a description of this work, which P.-M. Adéma kindly allowed me to consult, see his *Guillaume Apollinaire,* p. 293. The work itself consists of a typewritten version that is based on an unknown manuscript and that dates from after the poet's death. While it bears the note "Composé par Guillaume Apollinaire en 1916," the fact that this was added by a third person makes this date unreliable.

25. "Une lettre d'Apollinaire à Bakst," *Revue des Lettres Modernes,* nos. 183–188 (1968), special issue *Guillaume Apollinaire 7,* p. 178.

26. Adéma, *Guillaume Apollinaire,* p. 301.

27. Apollinaire may have taken this image from Marinetti, the author of *La Conquête des étoiles* (1902), who in 1909 referred to the Futurists as "artilleurs en goguette" ("exhilarated artillerymen") in a manifesto whose title is even more significant: *Tuons le clair de lune (Let's Kill the Moonlight).*

28. Letter from Giorgio de Chirico to Francesco Meriano dated 7 April 1918. Cited in Jannini, *La fortuna di Apollinaire,* pp. 73–74.

29. Guillaume Apollinaire, *Méditations esthétiques: les peintres cubistes,* ed. L. C. Breunig and J.-Cl Chevalier (Paris: Hermann, 1965), p. 46.

Chapter 7. Conclusion

1. The original text of *R. U. R. (Rossum's Universal Robots)* was published in Prague in 1920; the play itself was first performed there on 25 January 1921. Several critics have speculated that Capek's robots were inspired by the Golem legend associated with the Jewish quarter in Prague. For an interesting discussion of the Golem's relationship to other automata see Abraham Moles, "La Fonction des mythes dynamiques dans la construction de l'imaginaire social," *Symbols in Life and Art,* ed. James A. Leith (Kingston, Ont.: McGill-Queens University Press, 1987), pp. 77–87.

There is also a slight possibility that, like the mannequins, the robots may have their source in "Le Musicien de Saint-Merry." The Capek brothers were great admirers of Apollinaire and were certainly familiar with this poem. (See Vladimir Brett, "Apollinaire et les Tchèques," *Du monde européen à l'univers des mythes,* ed. Michel Décaudin [Paris: Minard, 1970], pp. 48–64.) It is important to note, however, that Capek's robots are neither faceless nor machinelike. Although they are mechanical contrivances, they are physically indistinguishable from their human masters.

Bibliography

Adéma, Pierre-Marcel. *Guillaume Apollinaire.* Paris: La Table Ronde, 1968.
Adhémar, Jean, et al., eds. *Apollinaire.* Paris: Bibliothèque nationale, 1969.
Agee, William. "New York Dada, 1910–1930." In *The Avant-Garde,* edited by Thomas B. Hess and John Ashberry, pp. 105–13. London: Collier-Macmillan, 1968.
Aisen, Maurice. "The Latest Evolution in Art and Picabia." *Camera Work,* special issue June 1913, pp. 14–21.
Anonymous. "Musique." *Nord-Sud,* nos. 4–5 (June–July 1971), p. 31.
———. "La Réforme coloniale," *Le Temps,* 13 January 1914.
Albert-Birot, Pierre. "Les Tendances nouvelles: interview avec Guillaume Apollinaire." *SIC,* nos. 8–10 (August–October 1916), pp. 2–3.
Apollinaire, Guillaume. "Albert Savinio et la nouveauté en musique." Signed "J. C." *Les Soirées de Paris,* nos. 26–27 (July–August 1914), pp. 369–70.
———. *Anecdotiques.* Edited by Marcel Adéma. Paris: Gallimard, 1955.
———. *A quelle heure un train partira-t-il pour Paris?* Edited by Willard Bohn. Montpellier, France: Fata Morgana, 1982.
———. *A quelle heure un train partira-t-il pour Paris?* Edited by Henrik van Scaldegem. Ghent, Belgium: Arteveld, 1986.
———. "Aquarelles de Picabia." Signed "L'Atelier." *Paris-Journal,* 29 May 1914, p. 3.
———. "L'Audition des oeuvres musicales de M. Albert Savinio." Signed "J. C." *Les Soirés de Paris,* no. 25 (15 June 1914), pp. 301–02.
———. *Chroniques d'art (1902–1918).* Edited by L. C. Breunig. Paris: Gallimard, 1960.
———. *L'Enchanteur pourrissant.* Edited by Jean Burgos. Paris: Minard, 1972.
———. "L'Esprit nouveau et les poètes." *Mercure de France,* vol. 130 no. 491 (1 December 1918), pp. 385–96.
———. "Francis Picabia." Signed "L'Atelier." *Paris-Journal,* 13 July 1914.
———. "G. de Chirico—Pierre Brune." *L'Intransigeant,* 30 October 1913.
———. Letter to Léon Bakst, 10 April 1917. "Une Lettre d'Apollinaire à Bakst," *Revue des Lettres Modernes,* nos. 183–88 (1968), series *Guillaume Apollinaire* 7, pp. 177–78.
———. *Lettres à Lou.* Edited by Michel Décaudin. Paris: Gallimard, 1969.
———. "Manuscrits et documents à la Bibliothique nationale." *Que Vlo-Ve?, Bulletin International des Etudes sur Apollinaire,* 2d ser., no. 12 (October-December 1984), pp. 8–11.
———. "Marius de Zayas." *Paris-Journal,* 19 July 1914.
———. *Méditations esthétiques: les peintres cubistes.* Edited by L. C. Breunig and J.-Cl. Chevalier. Paris: Hermann, 1965.

———. *Oeuvres complètes*. Edited by Michel Décaudin. 4 vols. Paris: Balland-Lecat, 1965–66.

———. *Oeuvres en prose*. Edited by Michel Décaudin. 3 vols. Paris: Gallimard: 1988–.

———. *Oeuvres poètiques*. Edited by Marcel Adéma and Michel Décaudin. Paris: Gallimard, 1965.

———. *Petites Flâneries d'art*. Ed. Pierre Caizergues. Montpellier, France: Fata Morgana, 1980.

———. *Le Poète assassiné*. Paris: Gallimard, 1947.

———. "Simultanisme-Librettisme." *Les Soirées de Paris*, no. 25 (15 June 1914), pp. 322–25.

———. *Souvenirs de la Grande Guerre*. Edited by Pierre Caizergues. Montpellier: Fata Morgana, 1980.

———. *Tendre comme le souvenir*. Paris: Gallimard, 1952.

———. "Le 30e Salon des Indépendants." *Les Soirées de Paris*, no. 22 (March 1914), pp. 183–88.

Bailey, Craig R. "The Art of Marius de Zayas." *Arts Magazine*, vol. 53, no. 1 (September 1978), pp. 136–44.

Baloche, Abbé. *Eglise Saint-Merry de Paris, histoire de la paroisse et de la collégiale 700–1910*. 2 vols. Paris: Oudin, 1911.

Bates, Scott. *Guillaume Apollinaire*. Rev. ed. Boston: Twayne, 1989.

———. *Guillaume Apollinaire*. Boston: Twayne, 1967.

———. *Petit Glossaire des mots libres d'Apollinaire*. Sewanee, Tenn.: privately printed, 1975.

Beale, S. Sophia. *The Churches of Paris*. London: Allen, 1893.

Beales, Derek. *The Risorgimento and the Unification of Italy*. London: Allen and Unwin; New York: Barnes and Noble, 1971.

Beattie, John. *Other Cultures: Aims, Methods, and Achievements in Social Anthropology*. New York: Free Press, 1964.

Blachère, Jean-Claude. *Le Modèle nègre: aspects littéraires du mythe primitiviste au XXe siècle chez Apollinaire—Cendrars—Tzara*. Dakar, Abidjan, and Lomé: Nouvelles Editions Africaines, 1981.

Bohn, Willard. "The Abstract Vision of Marius de Zayas." *The Art Bulletin*, vol. 62, no. 3 (September 1980), pp. 434–52.

———. *The Aesthetics of Visual Poetry, 1914–1928*. Cambridge: Cambridge University Press, 1986.

———. "Giorgio de Chirico and the Paradigmatic Method." *Gazette des Beaux-Arts*, vol. 106, nos. 1398–99 (July–August 1985), pp. 35–41.

———. "Giorgio de Chirico and the Solitude of the Sign." *Gazette des Beaux-Arts*, forthcoming.

———. "Metaphysics and Meaning: Apollinaire's Criticism of Giorgio de Chirico." *Arts Magazine*, vol. 55, no. 7 (March 1981), pp. 109–13.

———. "Phantom Italy: The Return of Giorgio de Chirico." *Arts Magazine*, vol. 56, no. 2 (October 1981), pp. 132–35.

———. "Picabia's 'Mechanical Expression' and the Demise of the Object," *The Art Bulletin*, vol. 67, no. 4 (December 1985), pp. 673–77.

———. "Sur la Butte: Apollinaire et Savinio." *Que Vlo-Ve?, Bulletin International des Etudes sur Apollinaire*, 2d ser., no. 13 (January–March 1985), pp. 5–9.
Madeleine Boisson, *Apollinaire et les mythologies antiques*. Fasano: Schena and Paris: Nizet, 1989.
Boudar, Gilbert et al. *La Bibliothèque de Guillaume Apollinaire*. 2 vols. Paris: CNRS, 1983 and 1987.
Breton, André. *Anthologie de l'humour noir*. Paris: Pauvert, 1966.
———. *Manifestes du surréalisme*. Paris: Gallimard, 1965.
———. *Oeuvres complètes*. Edited by Marguerite Bonnet et al. Paris: Gallimard, 1988–.
———. *Perspective cavalière*. Edited by Marguerite Bonnet. Paris: Gallimard, 1970.
———. *Le Surréalisme et la peinture*. Paris: Gallimard, 1928.
Breton, André and Gerard Legrand. *L'Art magique*. Paris: Club Français du Livre, 1957.
Brett, Vladimir. "Apollinaire et les Tchèques." In *Du monde européen à l'univers des mythes*, edited by Michel Décaudin, pp. 48–64. Paris: Minard, 1970.
Cailler, Pierre. *Guillaume Apollinaire: documents iconographiques*. Geneva: Cailler, 1965.
Caizergues, Pierre. *Apollinaire et "La Démocratie Sociale"*. Paris: Minard, 1969.
———. "Une Précision." *Revue des Lettres Modernes*, nos. 276–79 (1971), series *Guillaume Apollinaire* 10, pp. 113–14.
Čapek, Karel. *R. U. R. (Rossum's Universal Robots)*. Translated by Paul Selver. Garden City, N.Y.: Doubleday, 1923.
Carrà, Carlo. *Tutti gli scritti*. Edited by Massimo Carrà. Milan: Feltrinelli, 1978.
Carrà, Massimo et al. *Metafisica*. Milan: Mazzotta, 1968.
Carrieri, Raffaele. *Forme*. Milan: Milano-Sera, 1949.
———. *Iconografia italiana di Apollinaire*. Milan: Scheiwiller, 1954.
———. *Pittura e scultura d'avanguardia in Italia (1890–1955)*. Milan: Conchiglia, 1955.
Cendrars, Blaise. *Oeuvres complètes*. Paris: Denoël, 1963. 6 vols.
Chevalier, J.-Cl. and L. C. Breunig. "Apollinaire et *Les Peintres cubistes*." *Revue des Lettres Modernes*, nos. 104–7 (1964), series *Guillaume Apollinaire* 3, pp. 89–112.
Chirico, Giorgio de. *Hebdomeros*. Paris: Flammarion, 1964.
———. *Il meccanismo del pensiero: critica, polemica, autobiografia, 1911–1943*. Edited by Maurizio Fagiolo. Turin: Einaudi, 1985.
———. *Memorie della mia vita*. Milan: Rizzoli, 1962.
———. *Opera completa, 1908–1924*. Edited by Maurizio Fagiolo dell'Arco. Milan: Rizzoli, 1984.
Davies, Margaret. "Vitam Impendere Amori." *Revue des Lettres Modernes*, nos. 249–53 (1970), series *Guillaume Apollinaire* 9, pp. 69–93.
Dobbertin, Hans. *Quellensammlung zur Hamelner Rattenfängersage*. Göttingen: Schwartz, 1970.
Dulaure, J. A. *Des divinités génératrices chez les anciens et les modernes*. Paris: Mercure de France, 1905.
Durry, Marie-Jeanne. *Guillaume Apollinaire: "Alcools."* 3 vols. Paris: SEDES, 1956–1964.

Far, Isabella. *De Chirico*. Translated by Joseph M. Bernstein. New York: Abrams, 1968.
Follet, Lionel. "Apollinaire lecteur d'Empédocle." *Revue des Lettres Modernes*, nos. 576–81 (1980), series *Guillaume Apollinaire* 15, pp. 59–68.
Fongaro, Antoine. " 'Le vingt et un du mois de mai . . . ,' ". *Revue des Lettres Modernes*, nos. 380–84 (1973), series *Guillaume Apollinaire* 12, pp. 133–36.
―――. Review of Willard Bohn, *Apollinaire et l'homme sans visage*. *Rivista di Letterature Moderne e Comparate*, vol. 39 (1986), pp. 344–48.
Hillairet, Jacques. *Dictionnaire historique des rues de Paris*. Paris: Minuit, 1963.
Hugo, Victor. *Les Misérables*. Edited by Maurice Allem. Paris: Gallimard, 1964.
Hyland, Douglas. *Marius de Zayas: Conjuror of Souls*. Lawrence, Kans.: Spencer Museum of Art, 1981.
Jannini, P. A. *Le avanguardie letterarie nell'idea critica di Guillaume Apollinaire*. Rome: Bulzoni, 1971.
―――. *La Fortuna di Apollinaire in Italia*. 2d ed. Milan: Istituto Editoriale Cisalpino, 1965.
Jeanmaire, H. *Dionysos, histoire du culte de Bacchus*. Paris: Payot, 1951.
Jutrin, Monique. "La Présence du conteur dans la poésie d'Apollinaire." In *Regards sur Apollinaire conteur*, edited by Michel Décaudin, 9–21. Paris: Minard, 1975.
Lacassin, Francis. *Louis Feuillade*. Paris: Seghers, 1964.
Levaillant, Jean. "L'Espace dans *Calligrammes*." *Revue des Lettres Modernes*, nos. 217–22 (1969), series *Guillaume Apollinaire* 8, pp. 48–63.
Lockerbie, S. I. "Le Musicien de Saint-Merry." *Cahiers de l'Association Internationale des Etudes Françaises*, no. 23 (May 1971), pp. 197–209.
Marinetti, F. T. *La Conquête des étoiles: poème épique*. Paris: La Plume, 1902.
Martin, Marianne W. "Reflections on De Chirico and *Arte Metafisica*." *The Art Bulletin*, vol. 60, no. 2 (June 1978), pp. 342–53.
Moles, Abraham. "La Fonction des mythes dynamiques dans la construction de l'imaginaire social." In *Symbols in Life and Art*, edited by James A. Leith, 66–88. Kingston, Ont.: McGill-Queen's University Press, 1987.
Mollet, Baron. "Soirées à Paris et ballets russes avec Guillaume Apollinaire." *Les Lettres Françaises*, 11 November 1948, p. 3.
Nietzsche, Friedrich. *Sämtliche Werke*. Stuttgart: Kröner, 1964. 12 vols.
Nilsson, Martin P. *Geschichte der Griechischen Religion*. 2d ed. Munich: Beck'sche, 1955.
Paris, Renzo. "La volontà formativa nei 'Canti' di Alberto Savinio." *Quaderni del Novecento Francese*, no. 2 (1974), pp. 181–88.
Paz, Octavio. " 'The Musician of Saint-Merry' by Apollinaire: A Translation and a Study." Translated by Margaret Peden. *L'Esprit Créateur*, vol. 10, No. 4 (Winter 1970), pp. 269–84.
―――. *Traducción: literatura y literalidad*. Barcelona: Tusquets, 1971.
Philadelphia Museum of Art. *The Louise and Walter Arensberg Collection: Twentieth Century Section*. Edited by Fiske Kimball et al. Philadelphia, 1954.
Picabia, Francis. *Ecrits, 1913–1920*. Edited by Olivier Revault d'Allonnes. Paris: Belfond, 1975.

———. *Ecrits, 1921–1953 et posthumes.* Edited by Olivier Revault d'Allonnes and Dominique Bouissou. Paris: Belfond, 1978.

Piscopo, Ugo. *Alberto Savinio.* Milan: Mursia, 1973.

Pouillart, Raymond. "Apollinaire et quelques musiciens." In *Apollinaire et la musique*, edited by Michel Décaudin, pp. 55–62. Paris: Minard, 1967.

Poupon, Marc. "Le Musicien de Saint-Merry." *Cahiers de l'Association Internationale des Etudes Françaises*, no. 23 (May 1971), pp. 211–20.

Renaud, Philippe. *Lecture d'Apollinaire.* Lausanne: L'Age d'Homme, 1969.

———. "Le Musicien de Saint-Merry." *Cahiers de l'Association Internationale des Etudes Françaises*, no. 23 (May 1971), pp. 181–95.

———. "'Ondes,' ou les métamorphoses de la musique." In *Apollinaire et la musique*, edited by Michel Décaudin. Stavelot, Belgium: Les Amis de G. Apollinaire, 1967, pp. 21–32.

Rexroth, Kenneth. *Assays.* New York: New Directions, 1961.

Richter, Mario. "Apollinaire e le 'mordonnantes mériennes.'" *Studi Francesi*, no. 49 (January–April 1973), pp. 82–85.

Rognoni, Luigi. "Savinio musicista." In *Alberto Savinio*, edited by Franco Russoli. Electa, 1976, pp. 25–29.

Russoli, Franco, ed. *Alberto Savinio.* Milan: Electa, 1976.

Samaltanos, Katia. *Apollinaire: Catalyst for Primitivism, Picabia, and Duchamp.* Ann Arbor: UMI Research Press, 1984.

Sangiorgi, Giovanni and Jacopo Recupero, eds. *Omaggio ad Apollinaire.* Rome: Ente Premi Roma, 1960.

Sanouillet, Michel. *Dada à Paris.* Paris: Pauvert, 1965.

———. *Francis Picabia et "391".* Paris: Losfeld, 1966.

———. *"391," revue publiée de 1917 à 1924 par Francis Picabia.* Paris: Terrain Vague, 1960.

Savinio, Alberto. *Les Chants de la mi-mort. Les Soirées de Paris*, nos. 26–27 (July–August 1914), pp. 413–26.

———. *Les Chants de la mi-mort.* Paris: Parisot, 1938.

———. "Dammi l'anatema, cosa lasciva." *291*, no. 4 (June 1915), p. 4.

———. "Le Drame et la musique." *Les Soirées de Paris*, no. 23 (15 April 1914), pp. 240–44.

———. "In Poetae Memoriam." *L'Esprit nouveau*, no. 26 (October 1924), not paginated.

———. "Note." *Les Soirées de Paris*, no. 24 (15 May 1914), p. 246.

———. "Il poeta assassinato." *La Voce*, vol. 8, nos. 11–12 (31 December 1916), pp. 439–44.

———. "Scambi." *La Rassegna d'Italia*, vol. 1, no. 5 (May 1946), pp. 51–53.

———. *Vie des fantômes.* Translated by André Pieyre de Mandiargues et al. Paris: Flammarion, 1965.

———. *Vita dei fantasmi.* Milan: Scheiwiller, 1962.

Scott, George Ryley. *Phallic Worship.* London: T. Werner Laurie, 1941.

Shattuck, Roger. "The Aesthetics of Dada." *Dada/Surrealism*, no. 2 (1972), pp. 7–10.

Sloane, Joseph C. "Giorgio de Chirico and Italy." *Art Quarterly*, vol. 21, no. 1 (Spring 1958), pp. 3–22.
Smith, Philip. "Jedd Garet and the Atomic Age." *Arts Magazine*, vol. 55, no. 10 (June 1981), pp. 158–60.
Soby, James Thrall. *Giorgio de Chirico*. New York: Museum of Modern Art, 1955.
Soupault, Philippe. Preface, entitled "Quand Apollinaire contait . . . ," to *Les Epingles*, by Guillaume Apollinaire. Paris: Cahiers Libres, 1928.
Tzara, Tristan. *Oeuvres complètes*. Edited by Henri Béhar. 5 vols. Paris: Flammarion, 1975–82.
Weichsel, John. "Cosmism or Amorphism." *Camera Work*, nos. 42–43 (April–July 1913), p. 80.
Zayas, Marius de. "How, When, and Why Modern Art Came to New York." Edited by Francis M. Naumann. *Arts Magazine*, vol. 54, no. 8 (April 1980), pp. 96–126.
———. Letters to Alfred Stieglitz. Alfred Stieglitz Archive, Collection of American Literature, Beinecke Rare Book and Manuscript Library, Yale University
———. "Watch Their Steps." *291*, no. 3 (May 1915), p. 4.
Zoppi, Sergio. *Al festino di Esopo*. Rome: Bulzoni, 1979.

Index

Agee, William, 52
Aisen, Maurice, 52
Alighieri, Dante, 92, 109–12, 114, 158 n.43
Apollinaire, Guillaume, 13–15, 20, 137, 153; and African art, 22–23, 66–67; and Alberto Savinio, 47–50, 77–79, 87–88, 92–95, 98, 100, 113–14, 136–40; and Francis Picabia, 50–55, 141–44, 160 nn. 20 and 21; and Futurism, 70–74; and Giorgio de Chirico, 47, 86–88, 93, 96–104, 111–14, 117, 124–25, 137; and Marius de Zayas, 41–47, 77–80, 92–95, 132–34, 144–45. Works: *L'Antitradition futuriste*, 70; *A quelle heure un train partira-t-il pour Paris?* 13–14, 35, 41, 53–77, 79, 103–4, 117, 136–37, 141, 145–46, 158 n.1; "Arbre," 25, 102; "Banalités," 73; *Le Bestiare*, 35; *Case d'armons*, 144–45; "La Chanson du mal-aimé"; "Coeur couronne et miroir, 47, 49, 141; "Les Collines," 160 n.39; "Cors de chasse," 31; "Cortège," 22; "La Cravate et la montre," 133; "Un Dernier chapitre," 58–60; "Du Coton dans les oreilles," 147; "L'Emigrant de Landor Road," 74, 111–12; "Un Fantôme de nuées," 74; "Les Fenêtres," 103; *L'Homme sans yeux sans nez et sans oreilles*, 145–47, 166 n.24; "La Jolie Rousse," 75, 137–40; "Lettre-Océan," 46–47, 79, 133–34; "La Maison des Mortes," 22, 111; "Les Mamelles de Tirésias, 81, 95, 145–50; "Le Musicien de Saint-Merry," 13, 16–40, 63, 67–68, 74, 89, 133, 151, 153, 155 n.5, 155 n.8; "Océan de terre," 98; "Paysage," 47; "Les Peintres cubistes," 52, 150; "La Petite Auto," 132; "Poème lu au mariage d'André Salmon," 39, 157 n.27; "Le Poète assassiné," 30, 61–62, 73, 157 n.24; "Quelconqueries," 73; "Simultanisme-Librettisme," 132; *Souvenirs de la Grande Guerre*, 54–55; "Tour," 103; "Vendémiaire," 69, 103; "Voyage," 31, 34, 133, 145; "Zone," 22–23, 52, 103, 134
Apollinaire, Jacqueline, 98–100
Apollo, 34, 109–11, 120, 123
A quelle heure un train partira-t-il pour Paris?: and Picabia, 72–73, 141–44, 147–49; relation to *Les Chants de mimort*, 70, 74, 77, 84, 88–95, 117, 125; relation to *Les Mamelles de Tiresias*, 70, 75–76, 146–50; relation to "Le Musicien de Saint-Merry," 13, 41, 54, 55–56, 58–61, 64. *See also* Apollinaire, Guillaume: Works
Archipenko, Alexandre, 67
Arensberg, Walter Conrad, 52, 140–41, 165 n.16
Ariadne, 25, 35, 38–39, 87, 101–3, 109
Aristophanes, 37
Auric, Georges, 146

Bacon, Francis, 141
Bakst, Léon, 146
Baloche, Abbé, 156 n.10, 157 n.26
Bates, Scott, 34–35, 101, 157 n.22
Baudelaire, Charles, 29, 135
Beattie, John, 68
Blake, William, 120
Boccioni, Umberto, 72
Böcklin, Arnold, 112
Boisson, Madeleine, 34
Bosi, Carlo Alberto, 82
Botticelli, Sandro, 120
Breton, André, 13, 19, 40, 67, 123, 157 n.30, 162 n.7, 164 n.31; *Anthologie de l'humour noir*, 73, 82, 101, 104, 137; *Le Surréalisme et la peinture*, 100, 106–7

Cabinet des Dr. Caligari, Das, 154
Cailler, Pierre, 100
Caizergues, Pierre, 25
Calvocoressi, M. D., 49
Can Grande della Scala, 110
Čapek, Karel, 153, 166 n.1
Carles, Arthur B., 159 n.13
Carlo Alberto, 90–92, 107
Carrà, Carlo, 14, 72, 151, 163 n.11
Carrieri, Raffaele, 112–13
Catullus, 102
Cavour, Camillo Benso di, 90–92, 95, 107–12, 114, 136, 162 n.18
Cendrars, Blaise, 67
Cérusse, Jean, 50
Chirico, Andrea de. *See* Savinio, Alberto
Chirico, Giorgio de, 14, 35, 47, 54, 72; aesthetics, 100–131; and Apollinaire, 47, 86–87, 93, 96–104, 111–14, 117, 124–25, 137, 149–50; founder of Metaphysical Art, 14, 98, 151; and "Le Musicien de Saint-Merry," 101–3, 113–14, 117; relation to *Les Chants de la mi-mort,* 80–81, 86, 90–92, 113–17, 123–27; mannequins, 19, 101, 106–31, 136–37, 151–54; role in Surrealism, 14, 151. Works: *Apollinaire citaredo,* 98; *Ariadne,* 101; *The Child's Brain,* 106–7; *The Chimney,* 91, 103; *The Departure of the Poet,* 87; *The Destiny of the Poet,* 87, 93, 104; *The Disquieting Muses,* 110–11; *The Dream of the Poet* (see *The Nostalgia of the Poet); The Duo,* 115, 117, 127; *The Endless Voyage,* 114, 122–23, 125; *The Enigma of an Autumn Afternoon,* 112; *The Enigma of the Hour,* 97; *The Enigma of the Oracle,* 97, 112; *The Faithful Servitor,* 108, 111; *The Great Tower,* 100; *Hebdomeros,* 104–5; *Hector and Andromache,* 127, 130–31; *The Joy of Return,* 106; *I'll Be There . . . The Glass Dog,* 117–18, 120; *The Mathematicians,* 110–11; *Melanconia,* 102; *Mystery and Melancholy of a Street,* 93; *The Nostalgia of the Poet,* 118, 120; *Portrait of Guillaume Apollinaire,* 85–88, 93, 98, 100, 120, 123; *Portrait of His Brother Andrea,* 48; *Portrait of the Poet,* 87, 99–100, 120; *The Prophecy of the Scholar,* 127; *The Return,* 105–111; *The Return of the Poet,* 87; *The Sadness of Departure,* 97; *The Seer,* 127, 129; *Solitude,* 97; *Song of Love,* 119–20; *Still Life: Turin, Spring,* 104; *The Surprise,* 103; *The Torment of the Poet,* 121, 123, 125; *Troubador,* 127; *The Two Sisters,* 126; *The Vexations of the Thinker,* 127–28; "La Volonté de la statue," 112; *The Whistling of the Locomotive,* 97
Cocteau, Jean, 75–76
Coligny-Châtillon, Louise de, 140, 144
Copeau, Jacques, 71

Dali, Salvador, 151
Davies, Margaret, 157 n.21
Décaudin, Michel, 24
Delaunay, Robert, 103
Delvaux, Paul, 151–52
Diaghilew, Serge de, 50
Dionysos, 34–39, 66, 90, 102–3, 106–11, 114, 158 n.36, 158 n.39
Dobbertin, Hans, 157 n.27
Dodge, Mabel, 53
Duchamp, Marcel, 52, 141
Dulaure, J. A., 33, 37
Durry, Marie-Jeanne, 73

Empedocles, 158 n.43
Ernst, Max, 14, 151
Euripides, 36

Faceless man motif, the, 13–15, 151–54; and African sculpture, 66–67; in *A quelle heure un train partira-t-il pour Paris?,* 61–65; in Carlo Carrà, 151; in *Les Chants de la mi-mort,* 84, 86, 88–92; and *Fantômas,* 63–64; in Francis Picabia, 141–44; in Giorgio de Chirico, 101, 108–31, 151; in *Les Mamelles de Tirésias,* 149; in "Le Musicien de Saint-Merry," 27–29, 31–40; in Neo-Dada, 14; and Surrealism, 13–14, 19
Feuillade, Louis, 62–63
Fokine, Michel, 49–50
Fongaro, Antoine, 19, 82, 156 n.13, 157 n.25
France, Anatole, 106
Freud, Sigmund, 38

Garibaldi, Giuseppe, 90–92
Garet, Jedd, 14
Goethe, Johann Wolfgang von, 32
Golem, Der, 154
Golem, The, 154, 166 n.1
Griffith, D. W., 72
Grosz, George, 151
Guillaume, Paul, 47, 98, 100, 132, 137, 162 n.15, 163 n.21

Haviland, Paul B., 43
Heraclitus, 164 n.22, 164 n.35
Herodotus, 37
Hoffman, E. T. A., 154
Homer, 109, 120
Hugo, Victor, 156 n.13

Jannini, P. A., 72
Jarry, Alfred, 68, 70, 147

Kahnweiler, Daniel Henry, 132
Kerfoot, J. B., 134

Lamarque, General, 26
Lang, Fritz, 154
Laurencin, Marie, 24, 29–31, 33, 39
Lautréamont, Comte de, 162 n.7
Lawrence, D. H., 82
Levaillant, Jean, 64
Lockerbie, S. I., 22, 155 n.5

Magnelli, Alberto, 72
Magritte, René, 151
Mallarmé, Stéphane, 125
Marinetti, F. T., 70–71, 72–74, 147–48, 166 n.27
Matisse, Henri, 97
Mazzini, Giuseppe, 90–92
Meriano, Francesco, 162 n.16, 166 n.28
Mérimée, Prosper, 32
Meyer, Agnes Ernst, 133–34
Metaphysical School, 14, 98, 151
Metropolis, 154
Millet, Jean-François, 31
Milton, John, 120
Mollet, Jean, 60
Morandi, Giorgio, 14, 151
Munch, Edvard, 14

Napoleon III, 57–58, 68–70, 72, 104–11, 145

Nietzsche, Friedrich, 35–36, 80, 86, 102–3, 106, 110, 114, 162 n.11, 162 n.12, 165 n.19
Nilsson, Martin P., 158 n.36

Pagès, Madeleine, 103, 158 n.39
Palazzeschi, Aldo, 72
Papini, Giovanni, 72, 156 n.17
Paz, Octavio, 19, 22, 34
Petrarch, 109–11
Picabia, Francis, 14, 46–47, 137, 145, 152; and Apollinaire, 50–55, 141–44, 154, 160 n.20, 160 n.21; collaboration on *A quelle heure un train partira-t-il pour Paris?*, 41, 54–55, 62, 72–73, 77; *C'est de moi qu'il s'agit*, 53–54; Dada activities, 14, 72–73, 75, 134, 140–44; "Idéal doré par l'or," 141–42; *Jésus-Christ rastaquouère*, 143; "La Loi d'accomodation chez les borgnes," 154; *Mariage comique*, 53–54; *Marius de Zayas*, 42; and Marius de Zayas, 43, 52–54, 132, 134, 140, 159 n.13; "Poison ou revolver," 142–43; "Tambourin," 144
Picasso, Pablo, 21, 43, 46–47, 97
Pied Piper of Hamelin, The, 31–33, 35–36, 38, 60, 157 n.26, 157 n.27
Playden, Annie, 30
Poissonier, Bernard, 100
Pouillart, Raymond, 77
Poupon, Marc, 25–26, 29, 32–34, 38, 61, 157 n.23
Pratella, Balilla, 80

Racine, Jean, 102
Ramorino, General, 161 n.6
Rapp, Marie, 159 n.8
Read, Peter, 69
Reger, Max, 47
Renaud, Philippe, 23, 28, 34–35, 61, 157 n.21
Rexroth, Kenneth, 141
Rhoades, Katharine, 134
Richter, Mario, 34, 157 n.32
Rimbaud, Arthur, 120
Roché, Henri-Pierre, 141
Rognoni, Luigi, 95
Rousseau, Henri (The Douanier), 46–47, 55

Roussel, Raymond, 52
Russolo, Luigi, 70, 80

Satie, Erik, 146
Sanouillet, Michel, 135, 140
Sartre, Jean-Paul, 36
Savinio, Alberto, 14, 72, 109, 112, 137, 146, 153; and Apollinaire, 47–50, 77–79, 87–88, 92–95, 98, 100, 113–14, 136–40; avant-garde role, 14, 137; collaboration on *A quelle heure un train partira-t-il pour Paris?*, 41, 54–55, 61–62, 74, 77, 79; Dada activities, 134–36; and Marius de Zayas, 134–36; relation to *A quelle heure un train partira-t-il pour Paris?*, 70, 74, 77, 84, 88–95, 117, 125; relation to Giorgio de Chirico, 80–81, 86, 90–92, 96, 100–01, 113–17, 123–27; relation to *Les Mamelles de Tirésias*, 147–50. Works: "Bellovées fatales No. 12," 135; *Les Chants de mi-mort*, 50, 78, 80–95, 136–38; "Dammi l'anatema, cosa lasciva," 135; *Deux Amours dans la nuit*, 49; "Le Drame et la musique," 49, 78–79; "La festa muratoria," 165 n.8; *Hermaphrodito*, 80, 92, 123, 136; *Niobé*, 49, 80; "Note," 79; *Persée*, 49, 50; *Le Trésor de Rampsénit*, 49; *Vita dei fantasmi*, 113; "Un Vomissement musical," 137
Schlemmer, Oskar, 151
Scuola metafisica, 14, 98, 151
Shakespeare, William, 141
Sironi, Mario, 151
Soby, James Thrall, 98, 108, 113–14, 123
Soffici, Ardengo, 58, 72
Soler Casabon, 145–47

Soupault, Philippe, 156 n.9, 164 n.31
Stieglitz, Alfred, 41, 43, 52–55, 140, 159 n.8; correspondence with Marius de Zayas, 43–47, 132–33, 159 n.3, 159 n.13
Strauss, Richard, 35
Stravinsky, Igor, 79
Suger, Abbé, 26

Tanguy, Yves, 151
Tridon, André, 135
Tzara, Tristan, 75, 137, 161 n.44

Vergani, Orio, 137
Villiers de l'Isle Adam, Jean Marie Mathias Philippe Auguste, Comte de, 154
Villon, François, 25, 26, 30, 139–40
Vittorio Emanuele II, 81, 86, 90–92, 107, 162 n.12
Vollard, Ambrose, 46

Weichsel, John, 52
Whitman, Walt, 157 n.19

Zayas, Marius de, 14, 137, 146, 160 n.24; and Alberto Savinio, 134–36; and Apollinaire, 41–47, 77–80, 92–95, 132–34, 144–45; "At the Arden Gallery," 133; collaboration on *A quelle heure un train partira-t-il pour Paris?*, 41, 54–55, 62, 65–66, 132; correspondence with Alfred Stieglitz, 43–47, 132–33, 159 n.3; *Francis Picabia*, 45; and Francis Picabia, 43, 52–54, 132, 134, 140; *Guillaume Apollinaire*, 44; "Mental Reactions," 133; and *291* (magazine), 132–35, 145